T0320055

PROTECTIVE TARIFFS

Published for the International Finance Section
of the Department of Economics
and Social Institutions in Princeton University
Walker Foundation

•

PROTECTIVE TARIFFS

BY

FRANK D. GRAHAM

Princeton

PRINCETON UNIVERSITY PRESS

PROTECTIVE TARIFFS
FIRST APPEARED IN THE SERIES,
"CURRENT ECONOMIC PROBLEMS"
EDITED BY PAUL T. HOMAN

Printed in the United States of America

ISBN: 978-0-691-65367-9

CONTENTS

FOREWORD

SINCE the days of Adam Smith, during the whole period, that is, in which economics has been able to make any pretensions to scientific status, sentiment among economists has been overwhelmingly hostile to protective tariffs as a general and permanent policy. The economists' presentation of their case has, however, fallen on stony ground. Apart from some local and impermanent successes, their arguments have made little impression upon public opinion. In part, perhaps, this has been due to the form in which the arguments have been cast. There are sound reasons for avoiding a statement of the matter in terms of money, and economists have usually shunned doing so. But, unless the case is so stated, it is bound to seem unreal to those whose thinking on economic subjects is inevitably conditioned by the monetary medium in which they live, and move, and have their economic being. The present book, being intended not for mature economists but for a less expert audience, therefore approaches the matter from the monetary side. This does not smooth away all difficulties but it may help in an understanding of the elements of the matter.

There are dangers in any knowledge short of unattainable omniscience. Though it is by no means impossible to know that another man is wrong, no one can ever be fully sure that he himself is right. The reaction of economists against the popular fallacies associated with the protectionist appeal has perhaps, therefore, been carried too far. On the assumption that it has, the case for protection will here be presented with sympathy, though no support will be given to arguments which stand no chance of surviving scientific scrutiny.

A logically sound case can often be made for measures of protection which might secure a temporary trading advantage at the expense of foreign nations. Little weight, however, will be attached to such possibilities. If opportunities of this sort were not reciprocal, something might be said, on national grounds, for an attempt at realization of them wherever they were present. But they *are* reciprocal. For purely selfish if for no other reasons, therefore, the commercial policy of a great nation should avoid the tactics of a casual horse-trader and should compare in dignity with that of a solid private concern which expects to be in business indefinitely. A commercial policy worthy of the name must proceed on the basis of long-run considerations. The inability to see other than immediate effects has been responsible for many persistent and disastrous errors.

Legislation will always more or less closely reflect prevailing opinion in the constituencies from which the legislators come. The public is grossly misinformed on the elements of commercial policy and our tariff legislation is, in consequence, singularly bad. By far the most important part of our commercial policy is the protectionist system, but there is a scarcity of good elementary books devoted solely to this topic. Highly intelligent people without special training in economics have, therefore, no readily available corrective of the *naïveté* which one so often hears expressed. The present treatment may, perhaps, do something to fill this gap. The writer is acutely conscious of its defects but he has deliberately avoided the technicalities which a thoroughly comprehensive discussion would demand. One cannot develop philological concepts in a primer. No more can the niceties of what is, perhaps, the most complex branch of economic theory be expounded in a handbook. It is enough if the substance of scientific opinion can be conveyed. There has, even so, been a constant necessity of choosing between an unexceptional but esoteric statement and an exposition which will not be too technical for the lay reader. The writer has, to some extent, been impaled on both horns of this dilemma. He trusts, however, that the text will be reasonably clear, even to the uninitiated, and such refinements as are attempted have been put in footnotes and appendices. However poorly the task may have been done, he cherishes the hope that no reader of this book will henceforth fail to receive with scepticism the crude arguments with which we are persistently assailed, from both sides, in the press and platform discussion of protection.

It would be futile to attempt many acknowledgments but the impress of Professor F. W. Taussig of Harvard University, a great teacher, will always be present on anything I may do in the field of the present study. I have, however, gathered from innumerable more or less consciously apprehended sources. Most of the ideas expressed have long been common property. Reference to the work of others is therefore rare. This is not to deny borrowing. On the contrary, it has been so frequent as to preclude specific recognition.

F. D. G.

PROTECTIVE TARIFFS

CHAPTER I

INTRODUCTORY

MAGNA EST VERITAS SED ERRARE EST HUMANUM

TRUTH is mighty but it must wage an incessant and unequal war against well-nigh immortal error. There is, moreover, a marked difference in the character of this struggle in the social and in the physical sciences. In the *physical* sciences progress is steady; positions, once gained, are consolidated; errors, sloughed off, do not readily reappear; and every conquest is followed by further forward thrusts from a relatively assured and solid base. This is true both of the theory and of the practice, of the science and the art. In the *social* sciences, on the other hand, and particularly in economics, this is far from being the case. The *pure theory* of economics, it is true, like that of the physical sciences, proceeds fairly steadily from strength to strength, but the *art* persistently falters. Hampered by superstitions, perverted by ignorance posing as knowledge, crippled by dissensions among its practitioners, and lost in a welter of contradictory counsels, that art advances slowly at best and, time and again, loses ground already won.

The reason for this contrast between the mechanical and the economic arts is not far to seek. In the realm of physical phenomena, discussion is on a high plane;

no one asks, or receives, a hearing unless he is so conversant with the technology of his subject as to be worthy of some respect; the great mass of uninformed laymen are docile, and the rest are ignored. But in the realm of economics, the bulk of discussion is puerile; nearly everyone cherishes the illusion that he understands such matters; and one has but to find common ground in popular prejudices to be acclaimed "economist" by those who would be quite incapable of recognizing a real master of economic phenomena if they should stumble upon him.

The need for careful training in the technique of economic analysis is not understood by the general public as it is understood with respect to the problems of, let us say, physics or chemistry.[1] The world, in consequence, is filled with self-constituted economic experts, often with a considerable though meretricious reputation, who thrust their incongruous opinions on the more or less receptive masses. The humble men of whom these masses are composed, if left alone, would be quite incapable of the perversions to which they are often brought by blind leaders who believe themselves, and are believed, to be possessed of superior vision. In the natural sciences, moreover, where the influence of given factors can be isolated, erroneous action is ordinarily attended by evils which soon become unmistakably traceable to their true cause. In economic affairs, on the contrary, the effects of given causes are so obscured in the general medley of the effects of these and quite other factors, that economic medicine men can

---

[1] *Cf.* A. C. Pigou and D. H. Robertson, *Economic Essays and Addresses*, P. S. King and Son, Ltd., London, 1931, p. 6, for a discussion of this topic.

prosper, in honor, from age to age and, what is worse, can get their pernicious proposals adopted.

There is an almost universal tendency to confound sound business or political judgment with economic wisdom. The two things have, in fact, very little in common. A brilliant economist might, and probably would, make a very poor business man or politician; and successful men of business or politicians can be, and in fact almost always are, most incompetent guides in purely economic matters. It is true that economics and business deal with the same objective material. Business men, as such, however, inevitably base their economic judgments upon the criteria which are applicable to the success of an individual business concern. The true economist, on the other hand, must be trained to think in terms of the general welfare. The ordinary business point of view on economic matters is thus quite as naïve as is that of the theoretical economist on the details of business management.

ACADEMIC AND POPULAR JUDGMENTS ON COMMERCIAL POLICY

Nowhere, perhaps, is this contrast between the judgments of typical business men and those of economists more sharply drawn than in the field of commercial policy. That, for instance, an existing industry should be injured or eliminated by foreign competition is a bitter pill for the ordinary business man to swallow; yet, to the economist, it will frequently appear as a condition of the success of some alternative and better industry and of enlarged general prosperity. On a false analogy, again, with the affairs of a private business organization, the business man will think that a persistent "fa-

vorable" balance of international payments (which seems
to him the national counterpart of profits in his own
business) is indispensable to the economic happiness of
his country. The economist knows, however, that such
a balance is not only impossible but that it would be
undesirable if it could be achieved. To the business
man, exports are an end in themselves and imports a
more or less necessary evil. To the economist, on the
contrary, imports are the end and exports but the means
of acquisition of as large a volume of imports as foreigners can be induced to offer in exchange for the
exported goods. The business man will ordinarily put
the stigma of disloyalty upon a compatriot who buys
finished goods abroad on considerations of price and
quality alone.[2] The economist, however, is alive to the
fact that every purchase of foreign goods *inevitably*
creates a market for future, or is the correlative of past,
exports from his own country, and that, in general,
restraints upon the freedom to purchase in the most
favorable market will injure not only the consumers
but also export producers in the country imposing the
restrictions. The business man (and with him the laborer) looks upon imports as a cause of unemployment
and of a lowered scale of living, but rigorous logic leads
the economist to the conviction that, in the long run,
restrictions upon imports provoke at least as much unemployment as they banish and that, far from preventing a fall in standards of living, they are a cause thereof. Finally, the business man (in the United States at
any rate) thinks of low foreign wages as a cause of
low money costs of production, but to the economist
it is evident that such low wages are a result of low

---

[2] Note, for example, the campaign to "Buy British" in the former
stronghold of free trade.

productivity and that they are, as often as not, accompanied by very high money costs per unit of output.

Such contrasts in point of view could be multiplied indefinitely. Enough has been said, however, to show that just as, in spite of what "common sense" would lead us to believe, the sun does not move round the earth, so the views on commercial policy, even of imposing figures in business and political life, are often as distorted as those of the able leaders of the Inquisition in their opposition to Galileo. In the economic as in the physical world the obvious explanation is nearly always wrong. For this reason we shall find that most of the popular arguments for protection are fallacious, while such arguments for a system of restraints as are logically valid seldom find a place in ordinary discussion.

THEORY VS. HISTORY AND STATISTICS

The problems of commercial policy must, in the main, be handled deductively since history and statistics throw a most uncertain light upon them. The march of events, after a given policy has been put into effect in one country or another, can of course be determined with some approach to accuracy, but it would be vain to imagine that those events were the necessary result of that policy. One can never know what would have happened if the opposite policy had been adopted. To take a specific example, we may note the extraordinary forward spurt in British trade, production, power, and prosperity after the adoption of the free trade policy in 1846, but it is open to an opponent of free trade to assert that this would have occurred in any case and to point to the equally remarkable crescendo in American economic life under high, and generally increasing, protection.

If, moreover, we look at the status of countries in general, under one system or the other, we shall find that, under high protection, certain countries are in the van of prosperity with others wretchedly poor, and that this is almost equally true of countries which have low, or no, protective duties. To revert to historical data, we may note that the rate of economic progress in the United States appears on the whole to have been not much greater or less under the approach to a free trade system which marked the period 1833 to 1861 than it has been in periods characterized by the opposite commercial policy.

If, in this matter, we could learn anything from history our provisional conclusions might then be: (1) that commercial policy is of but slight significance to the prosperity of any given country, or (2) that different policies are appropriate to different times and places. Both of these conclusions have, in fact, something of truth and a good deal of error in them. As far as the former of them is concerned, it should be recognized that the importance of a sound foreign commercial policy, though by no means insignificant, has been greatly exaggerated by partisans of both the *laissez-faire* and the restrictionist schools. Prosperity is dependent upon a complex of factors of which commercial policy is, in most cases, by no means the most important. In the case of a poor country the best possible foreign commercial policy might lift the nation but slightly above the low level of income which was due to other factors in the situation, and a very bad foreign commercial policy might not prevent another nation from enjoying most of the fruits of an otherwise favorable conjuncture. This is the more true, in both cases, in the degree in which the nation in question is a microcosm substantially reproducing within its borders the relationship between the factors of production which prevails in the world as a whole. Where, on the other hand, the national deviation from such world relationships is wide, sound foreign commercial policy is of great significance.

Referring now to the second provisional conclusion from history, that different policies are appropriate to different times and places, it will be enough here to say that the element of truth which it contains has usually been stretched beyond all reason by opponents of the classical free trade doctrines. Their interest has usually been anything but scientific. The fact is that there are certain principles in the field of foreign commercial policy which can be laid down, without hesitation, as valid *in all times and places*. There are, on the other hand, special circumstances in which the usual corollaries of those principles should not be drawn with rigor, or should be discarded. What these circumstances are it will be the principal object of this book to discover.

CHAPTER II

THE NATURE OF PROTECTION

THE United States permits the import of coffee, raw silk, rubber, and many other products, free of duty. These products could, at a pinch, be produced within the borders of the Union and *would* be so produced if a sufficiently high protective tariff were imposed upon their entry. All of the reasons ordinarily alleged for the imposition of protection apply. The commodities mentioned are produced in their countries of origin by workers who are paid only a tithe of the current American rate of wages. Their free import prevents the setting up of industries in this country or limits the demand for the products of indirectly competitive industries already established here. If, behind a tariff wall, production of these commodities should be started in this country, much new employment would be given and the workers engaged would furnish a market for the products of other domestic industries. And so on. It is true that there is no present domestic production of these goods. They are therefore not directly competitive with our own output, but this is solely because we have not provided protection. There would be no domestic production of many other commodities if we had not sheltered them.

8

Why do we make exception of certain goods? Why do we completely forget, with respect to them, the allegedly scientific principle on which American tariffs are supposed to be based, that of equalizing costs of production at home and abroad?[1] Why do we seek to get these commodities as cheaply as possible while shutting out others on the ground that they are being sold below the American cost of production?[2] Why, in a word, do we not carry protection to its logical conclusion?

The answer which would ordinarily be given to the question just raised is that, in applying protection, we must be reasonable. It is clear to all save fanatics that it would not be "worth while" for us to grow our own coffee, raw silk, and rubber. Why then is it worth while to grow at home a sizable proportion of our supply of sugar and most of our wool of certain kinds, and to manufacture pottery, laces, etc., when we could obtain them more cheaply abroad? What is the rule of reason in the matter?

Effective protection always tends to make not only the levying country but other countries more self-sufficing. If the United States should levy protective duties upon silk, rubber, and coffee, and, in consequence, proceed to grow its own supply, the producers of those

---

[1] This is the phrase ordinarily used. A tariff, of course, cannot equalize cost of production. What is meant is the addition of a charge (duty) to the foreign cost of production which will make the price of an import delivered to the American market at least equal to the cost of a similar article produced in the United States.

[2] We have, at one time or another, ardently protested against devices for raising the prices of all of the commodities named, yet these, or still higher prices, would have favored domestic production. At the very moment that these protests were being made, moreover, we were seeking to exclude other commodities on the allegation that they were being sold to us too cheaply.

commodities in Japan, Malaysia, Brazil and other countries, having lost their American market, would be compelled to resort to other pursuits and not improbably would undertake the production of wheat, cotton, or manufactured commodities which they now import from the United States. Our foreign market for wheat, cotton, and certain manufactured commodities having then been lost or curtailed, we should simply have exchanged one industry for another.

A given number of American workers, however, will not be able to produce directly as great an amount of coffee, silk, or rubber as they would have obtained by producing the other commodities for which they had formerly secured coffee, silk, and rubber in exchange. Similarly a given number of foreigners will not be able to produce directly as much wheat, cotton, or manufactured goods as they would have obtained had free trading relations made it possible for them to concentrate on coffee, silk, and rubber, and, with the money proceeds thereof, buy the commodities which they will otherwise be impelled to produce at home.[3] Both Americans and the foreigners will lose. In the case assumed this is so clear as to require no emphasis. Thoroughgoing self-sufficiency could obviously not be attained except at extreme cost. But where is the line to be drawn? What products is it desirable to produce at home, and in what measure for each product? If it is clearly foolish to protect industries which, if they are

---

[3] Even if the foreigners, as a result of the exclusion of their original products from the American market, do not shift to the production of American exports, they will be forced into lines which will curtail the exports of a third group of countries. This third group of countries will then be compelled to take up the production of goods hitherto obtained from the United States. In any event the United States loses an export market.

to be pursued in the United States, need duties of at least 1000 per cent, what shall we say of industries which need 500, 100, 50, or merely 5 per cent?

DISCRIMINATORY CHARACTER OF PROTECTION

No intelligent decision as to what is a reasonable duty can be made until it is realized that effective protection is, in its nature, discriminatory, and that every duty has its cost. It is impossible to "protect" one industry without, at the same time, injuring other industries in the same country. Congress cannot grant tariff favors except by taking from some what it gives to others. Through import duties we can offer shelter to certain producers against foreign competition. We cannot by this means, however, protect export industries. Such industries are bound to meet foreign competition and, for the reasons above given, they will find that such competition is greatly increased through the protective duties levied by their own country on other products. The result will be that such industries will decline or, when the general movement of economic life is upward, will fail to expand as rapidly as would otherwise be the case.

Furthermore, the great group of occupations including construction, transportation, communication, wholesale and retail trade, service industries, education, the professions, and many others, which are neither subject to foreign competition from imports nor engaged in production for export, cannot be favored by import duties; on the contrary, in so far as a larger part of the national income is devoted to securing at enhanced cost the commodities which can be and are, in fact, protected, these industries will find their own markets narrowed.[4] To protect one group of industries, therefore, is to expose others to an increasingly bitter wind.

It is often supposed that protection can be made universal, but this is an illusion. The attempt to widen protection to include all existing industries would render it completely ineffective and would establish essentially free trade conditions though at a higher all-round price level. All industries are in competition with one another for labor and for markets. One group may be favored at the expense of others, but it is not possible to favor all. To seek to do so is analogous to giving all competitors in a foot race the same handicap. Farmers and other exporters are no doubt entitled, in equity, to a bonus on their exports equal to the benefit which such industries as would otherwise be open to foreign competition in the home market receive from protection. Bounties on export or similar devices, as a fair counterpart to protective import duties, require, however, expensive administrative machinery to attain the same real result as could be secured, under a regime of complete free trade, without any machinery at all. The economic structure would be the same in both cases, but the internal price level in the country adopting the tariff plus bounty system would be high relative to that of the rest of the world. The prices of imports would be raised (in the domestic market) by the amount of the tariff duties, while those of exports would be raised (in the domestic market) by the amount of the bounties. The product of industries putting out goods consumed at home would, in the play of competition, eventually sell at equivalent prices. With every-

---

[4] The greater the share of the national income paid for artificially protected commodities, the less there is for the products of other employments.

body paying as well as receiving high prices, all would be in the same real situation as would obtain under the lower free trade price level. Foreigners, in their turn, would be offering goods to, and receiving goods from, the "protected" country at the lower level which would correspond with their own internal price structure. If the system could be so developed as to remove all discrimination the volume and composition of exports, of imports, and of domestic production and consumption, apart from a diminution proportional to the expense of administration, would be precisely the same as if neither import nor export duties had ever been levied. The same amount would be expended on export bounties as was collected on import duties, and no import duty or export bounty could justly be set at any figure which would promote or limit such influx or efflux of the commodity in question as would occur under perfectly free competition.

Such a removal of discrimination would, it is clear, automatically remove protection. Disregarding foreign action, it would then be no more or less difficult for Americans to sell in foreign markets (or for foreigners to sell in the domestic market) than it would be if imports were free of any charge. It would, of course, be the height of folly, through clumsy and costly governmental machinery thus to attain an end which might be realized without any machinery at all; but it must be admitted that it is sometimes better to answer a fool according to his folly than to seek to confound him with the most perfect logic.

Discrimination, however, is not necessarily bad; it may be the highest wisdom. The real point at issue is how, if at all, to discriminate, and to what degree. Different forms of discrimination in tariff policy have different effects. This is clearly brought out in the contrast between protective and revenue duties. The two are mutually inconsistent. In so far as a duty yields revenue it is not protective, and in so far as it is protective it yields no revenue. Any given duty may, indeed, be a compromise. The import duty on sugar in the United States may be cited as an example. As far as imports continue over the duty the government obtains revenue but the protection is, by the same token, incomplete. As far, on the other hand, as the duty is effective in excluding foreign supplies and promoting production at home, there is a measure of protection but there is no revenue. Free trade countries, such as Great Britain in the pre-war period, may therefore obtain much greater revenues from import duties than do protectionist countries. A completely protectionist country would, in fact, obtain from import duties no revenue at all. Conversely, the greatest revenue could be obtained from import duties in which there is no element of protection.

To preserve the character of revenue duties any import levy, which would otherwise promote domestic production at the expense of imports of the commodity in question, must be accompanied by an equivalent excise tax. Revenue duties are one form of taxation. They are a discrimination against such products as are singled out for taxation but not as between different sources of supply. The consumer pays an enhanced price for his product and the differential charge accrues to the Treasury. Protective duties impose a similar burden on the consumer but no corresponding receipt appears in the Treasury's accounts. Protective duties may perhaps, therefore, be regarded as taxation but, if so, they are taxation without revenue. If revenue were the object of American tariff policy, duties would be levied on the very products which now come in free—such as tea, coffee, silk, rubber, and tin—and would be lowered on those products which are now excluded and produced at home. The essence of a practical free trade policy is not lack of tariff taxation or even lack of discrimination, since all special taxation is to some extent discriminatory, but absence of that type of discrimination which distinguishes directly between producers at home and abroad, and indirectly between the domestic producers of the protected and other commodities, and by so doing substantially alters the composition of the national industry in a generally noxious manner.

THE BASIS OF PROTECTION

Since there is no fiscal compensation for the discrimination involved in protective tariffs, such discrimination must be justified as inherently beneficial. The imposition of protective duties, however, means that the levying nation, as a whole, tends to buy certain commodities at higher prices and to sell others at lower.[5] This, in itself, is no way to get rich. The higher prices will, it is true, be paid to domestic producers; but such producers do not make extraordinary profits since their costs are so great that, in the absence of protection, they would prefer to engage in other activities. Such higher prices as are paid for imports and such lower prices as are received for the national exports are therefore without present compensation. Domestic producers of the protected commodity get a larger market but domestic

---

[5] This follows from the contraction of the market for export industries which the exclusion of imports involves.

producers of exports find their market narrowed. The net immediate result is a loss.

Opponents of protection base their case not on the fact that protection is discriminatory but that the discrimination is worse than futile, that it involves gratuitous waste. The argument can be successfully met only if it can be shown that the immediate disadvantage is compensated by ulterior benefits. All protective duties are costly in the present, but some may yield compensating advantages in the future. No approximation to other than a naïve policy is possible without a careful estimate of the relative weight of these present and future factors, or without precise notions as to the industries it is good for the nation to have, the share in the national economic structure which each should hold, and the cost of changing the composition of the national industry. To these considerations we shall return in a later chapter.

The very name "protection" has a comforting but misleading connotation. If we should call protection what it is, discrimination, and should recognize that this discrimination immediately affects adversely not only the foreign producer of the commodities concerned but also the great bulk of domestic producers who cannot be protected, as well as practically all domestic consumers, we should then regard the matter with clear eyes instead of through a fog of unwarranted hope, fear, and favorable prejudice. The case turns entirely on possible eventual compensations of the present loss.

CHAPTER III

CRITIQUE OF POPULAR, AND FALLACIOUS, ARGUMENTS FOR PROTECTION

PROTECTION, EMPLOYMENT, AND THE STANDARD OF LIVING

THE plea that protection is essential as a safeguard of a high standard of living, and as a preventive of unemployment, is politically potent but almost wholly fallacious. The real issues involved in protection can profitably be discussed only after these false views have been dismissed. The naïve acceptance of such views arises from illusions with regard to the relationship between wages and prices, to the real sources of prosperity, and to the causes of unemployment.

If we reflect that the national standard of living is absolutely conditioned by the national output *plus* imports *minus* exports, that, with a given national monetary income, high prices reflect not prosperity but adversity, and that unemployment is no greater a problem in countries with a liberal than in those with a restrictive commercial policy, we shall not easily fall into the error of approving a *general* restriction of imports, a general raising of prices without corresponding increase in money incomes, and the building up of certain industries at the inevitable expense of others to which we are better adapted.

Clarity of thought on these matters is furthered when we take a genetic view of the development of our economy and note that, with the increasing complexity of economic life, there has occurred one of those perversions of thought in which emphasis comes to be laid upon means to the exclusion of the ends they were originally designed to serve.

When the American colonies were first settled communication with Europe was so difficult, uncertain, and commercially profitless, that the pioneers were forced into self-sufficiency. The ideal of isolation, whatever its worth, was then rather fully realized. The colonists, however, were far from satisfied. If, in their religion and politics, they desired only to be let alone, they were by no means of the same mind when it came to trade. On the contrary, as soon as transport and trade could be developed, they cheerfully abandoned some of their activities in order to concentrate all of their productive powers in lines in which they, and their new country, were most apt. A monetary system, in the European understanding of the term, hardly existed—barter was prevalent—but it was obviously advantageous to specialize upon the production of those things which, after allowing for cost of transfer, could be sold in Europe, or elsewhere, for more money than need there be given for other goods which could be produced in the colonies only at higher cost than that expended on the exports.

There were definite human and material resources available. The task of the colonists was to use them to the best advantage. The problem was solved solely by consideration of prices in foreign markets *relative* to cost in the colonies. If units of transportable goods, which required a given outlay to produce at home, were selling for varying prices abroad, it was clear gain to abandon the domestic production of such of these goods as were selling at relatively low prices in foreign markets so that the conserved productive power might be applied to those which were selling at a higher figure; to continue this process as long as price differences existed; and to secure in trade, at low prices, the commodities on which production was being abandoned. It made not the slightest difference what the *absolute* prices in foreign markets happened to be or what were the absolute costs of production in the colonies.[1] Trade was in any event the means of obtaining the maximum real income, the way to have more of every good than could otherwise be secured.

If there were any unemployed the clearly sensible thing was that they should work, along with their fellows, at those things which commanded high prices in foreign markets relative to cost of production at home, rather than that, as a result of the exclusion of imports

---

[1] Suppose that the prices, in English markets, of a unit of wheat and a unit of nails, each of which could be produced at equal cost in the colonies, were £2 and £1 respectively. It would be clearly advantageous for the colonists to specialize in wheat and import nails. It would be equally advantageous to do so should the prices in English markets fall to, let us say, £1 and £½ respectively, or should rise to £4 and £2. The same is true, if, as a result of technical or other changes, the cost of production in the colonies should fall for both commodities to one-half, or any other fraction, of its former level or rise to any common multiple thereof. Without a clear grasp of the fact that *absolute* price and cost levels are irrelevant to the theory of trade, that it is only *relationships* between individual prices that matter, confusion and error are inevitable. Absolute prices, of course, determine trade carried on under anything like free conditions. But this is only because trade in money itself brings international price *levels* into such approximation to equality as to make absolute and relative prices substantially the same thing. The present discussion of course applies only to such goods as are not rendered immobile by prohibitively great artificial restrictions on movement.

of relatively low-priced goods, they should enter upon the production thereof.[2] Since the workers, under the circumstances posited, could not produce as much of the hitherto imported commodities as could have been obtained in exchange for the exports they might otherwise have turned out, the general standard of living must, for the time being at any rate, have suffered a reduction on the adoption of a policy of restraint of imports.

The general standard of living in the colonies and in foreign countries, though affected by commercial policy, was, like absolute prices, a factor of no significance in determining what that policy should be. In the beginning the colonists' standard of living was very greatly below that of the European countries with which they carried on trade. When later it rose, the change had no bearing on the benefits from the overseas trade. As time went on, inventions, improvements, changes in demand, or the necessity for using poorer resources as the production of any one commodity in any one area was extended, altered, on both sides of the water, the costs and prices of the various commodities exchanged, and affected the composition and even the direction of overseas trade, but did not affect the fundamental principle above laid down.

Far from rejecting imports because they were cheap, the colonists were served by Yankee traders who combed the markets of the world with the rational objective of securing importable goods as cheaply as possible. The

---

[2] The picture of colonial life and policy given in this chapter is an idealization not meant to be historically accurate. It presents, I think, the *trend* of events; but the path to economic realism in the colonies, as elsewhere, was obstructed by traditional modes of thought inherited from the former environment of the settlers. *Cf.* E. A. J. Johnson, *American Economic Thought in the Seventeenth Century*, P. S. King & Son, Ltd., London, 1932.

colonists were calmly indifferent to foreign wages, conditions of labor, and standards of living. They knew that their own standard of living was not conditioned by that of foreigners but was a resultant (1) of their own productive skill and resources, and (2) of trading shrewdly at as high prices for exports and as low prices for imports as could be attained. They were not afraid of imports or of the competition of low-wage labor. The freest of trade could not rob them of their efficiency and, whatever the wages and standards of living of other peoples might be or become, they knew that their own welfare was dependent upon their own productive efforts. The principle still holds.

NATIONAL PRICE STRUCTURES AND INTERNATIONAL EXCHANGE

Proceeding from barter to the use of such media of exchange as wampum, which had no currency in the Old World, the pioneers still had but little opportunity for direct comparison of national price structures. There was, consequently, small room in their minds for the false notions that high wages make high prices and that a rich country will somehow be ruined by trading with a poor one. The price *level* in the New World was divorced from that of the Old World, and both were a matter of complete irrelevance in international trade. It was only the variation of *individual* prices, within either price structure, which was of significance. Whether each of two commodities cost 10 or 1000 strings of wampum in the colonies was as irrelevant as was the absolute price level in foreign countries. Whatever the absolute height of foreign prices might be, if only the two commodities did not sell in foreign markets at the same *relative* price as at home, it paid the pioneers, and the Europeans, to concentrate on the production and export of those goods which, relative to other articles, were reciprocally more valuable in foreign markets than in their own.

Under the lower of the colonial price levels in the above supposition colonial traders would lay out 10 strings of wampum per unit of export; sell their stock in foreign markets; buy, with the foreign currency proceeds, a *larger number of units* of the commodity relatively cheap in the foreign center; dispose of them in the colonial market at 10 wampum strings per unit, and thus make a wampum profit *pro rata* with the percentage difference in the foreign price of the two commodities. The same principle applies equally well to the higher of the two price levels. The trade could, of course, be conducted with equal advantage by foreign as by colonial merchants, and the price structure which made it advantageous for the inhabitants of one country to concentrate on the production of the one commodity made it equally advantageous for others to concentrate on the alternative.

In lieu of round-trip trading under a single entrepreneur, specialization in exporting, importing, and transportation soon made its appearance. This specialization called for an exchange of currencies. Since wampum was a valid medium of exchange only in the colonies, the amount of foreign currency offered for a unit thereof depended upon the general commodity purchasing power of wampum as compared with foreign currency units. Its precise foreign currency value at any given moment settled at the point at which the demand for, and supply of, wampum against foreign currencies, and therefore of foreign currencies against wampum, were in equilibrium. Foreign currency demand for wampum came from the possessors of foreign currencies who wanted to make purchases in the colonies, and the supply of wampum against foreign currencies from such colonists as wanted to make purchases abroad. The equilibrium momentarily established would be stable only when the rate of exchange tended to provoke a persistent equality between both the wampum and the foreign exchange value of the total of maturing claims and counterclaims arising from international transactions.

If the foreign exchange value of total imports tended to exceed the foreign exchange value of total exports, the rate at which wampum would sell against foreign currencies would decline. This would make colonial products cheaper to foreign purchasers and Old World products dearer to the colonists, would expand colonial exports and contract colonial imports, until equilibrium in the foreign exchange and the wampum value of total exports and imports was achieved. The opposite tendency of total exports to exceed total imports would be corrected by an enhancement of the foreign currency price of wampum with attendant effects the contrary of those just described but also leading to equilibrium.

The course of exchange rates would thus show minor fluctuations about a norm which represented the respective current general purchasing powers of the currencies involved. Whenever the purchasing power of wampum and foreign currencies changed *relative to one another*, the norm would alter, but there would have been no such tendency if they had changed in equal degree and in the same direction.

The pioneers were much too eager for consumable

goods to store up dead assets in silver and gold. The precious metals, whenever acquired, were therefore shipped out as a means of payment for imports. When the need for a money more convenient than wampum, or like substitutes, made itself felt, recourse was had to inconvertible paper monetary media, the changing foreign exchange value of which was determined in essentially the same manner as has just been described for wampum. The same principles are, of course, applicable to the inconvertible paper currencies now so widely in use.

Eventually, however, silver was more or less definitely established as currency in the colonies or in the states which evolved therefrom. Some English coin was used, but Spanish currency soon became dominant and continued to be employed in this country long after the Revolution. The Spanish coins were also current not only in Spain but in most of South America, the West Indies, and other countries. The North American settlers of course sold their exports at as high prices in Spanish silver as they could get, and they diverted the supply of any given commodity from the domestic to the foreign market, or *vice versa*, until the net returns, in Spanish silver, from a sale at home and abroad were equal. Imports, on the other hand, were obtained from foreign producers who were pursuing the same policy.

The wholesale price *level* of mobile goods[3] in the various colonies was thus brought into a fixed relationship of substantial equality with the similar price level in other countries using the same or allied currencies, some commodities being priced lower (exports) and

---

[3] These are the only prices which have any direct bearing on international trade.

others higher (imports) in any one of the countries with respect to the others.[4] The use of the same currency as was employed in other countries made the colonial price level of mobile goods part of a world system to which it was automatically tied. It could neither rise substantially above, nor fall substantially below, this world price level.

The Spanish coins came into the North American colonies only because the settlers preferred to take some of the proceeds of their exports in this form rather than in directly consumable commodities. Whenever this was overdone, however, the colonists, having plenty of silver, would bid higher silver prices for both domestic and imported commodities, while the inhabitants of the other countries using the same currency, an excessive part of which had now moved to North America, would bid lower silver prices for all types of products.

The result was that the North American colonists not only obtained, for the moment, a larger share of their own output, and thus left less for export, but they also obtained a larger share of the commodity output of other countries in the form of imports. This alteration in the ratio of commodity exports to imports called for an efflux of coins from North America in payment for the relatively enlarged commodity import and, through this efflux of coins, the whole process was reversed. The trend toward deviation of one price *level* from a position of substantial equality with others could clearly then not proceed very far in either direction.

---

[4] The difference in price from one country to another was approximately equal to the cost of transfer of the commodity between the two markets. Mobile commodities not actually transferred of course differed in price in the two markets by something less than this amount.

While wholesale commodity price *levels* of mobile goods were substantially equal in all the countries using a common medium of exchange, wages and other money incomes varied greatly from one country to another. The North American colonists were selling in foreign markets certain commodities which were being produced in, and exported from, other parts of the world. All sellers in any given market had, of course, to take the same price for goods of like quality. The *monetary return* to the producer was therefore proportionate to his *productivity*, and this was reflected in wage rates.

The transition from the monetary systems above described to those now in use was almost insensible and involved no new principles. After the formation of the United States bimetallism was established, with a national silver and gold coinage based on the Spanish dollar which continued to be widely used. The price structure was determined substantially as in the past, though national metal monetary units, instead of moving freely in unchanged form from circulation in one country to circulation in another, were first melted and then recoined. However, exchange rates between metallic currencies represented the respective weight of metal in the currency units, and national wholesale price levels of mobile goods, measured in any given weight of silver (any silver currency), maintained their relationship of substantial equality practically unchanged. Bimetallism in this country gave way to the gold monometallic standard to which most of the world, following the example of England, adverted during the nineteenth century. The principles of international price determination under an international gold standard, however, are the same as they were under silver. Under inconvertible paper standards, they are much the same as under wampum.

The price structure in any internationally trading country is thus linked with a world price system. It is a condition of the maintenance of the gold standard in any country that the gold wholesale price level of mobile goods shall not rise above the similar price level in other nations by even the slight amount which would bring *permanent* disequilibrium between total imports and total exports other than gold. If no adequate action is taken by banking authorities to prevent such a rise, the eventual inevitable abandonment of the gold standard might leave prices high, or even increasing. The monetary unit, however, would then fall in gold value, and in the rate at which it would exchange against foreign gold currencies, to a point at which the existing domestic price level, at the then current rates of exchange, would bear the same relationship to foreign gold or paper prices as if the country in question, and all other countries concerned, were still upon a gold currency basis. The same principles thus apply, whatever the character of national monetary systems.[5]

As long, therefore, as *any* foreign trade persists, the countries from and to which goods move will have interdependent price structures, with the wholesale price levels of mobile goods, measured in any given currency, substantially equal. This tendency is wholly automatic. The prevailing opinion that countries of high wages are countries of high prices, and countries of low wages countries of low prices, is quite without foundation. National wholesale commodity price levels of mobile goods

---

[5] For a more detailed analysis of price and wage structures, see Appendix I.

are fixed in a substantially equal relationship to one another by that equilibrium of total exports and imports imposed by the necessity of giving a *"quid"* for a *"quo."*[6] Other commodity prices are linked with this international price level and vary inversely with the effectiveness of domestic, relative to export, industries in each country.

WAGE STRUCTURES

Wages are the resultant of earning power *within* the international price system as a datum. Money wages are not a cause but an effect of prices *cum* productivity. The absolute height of prices and wages is irrelevant to national prosperity, once all adjustments have been made to a given price and wage structure. The significant thing is the *relationship* between the said prices and wages. Prices in all countries, when measured in any common medium, fluctuate together in approximately the same degree and direction.[7] National wholesale price levels of

---

[6] Much confusion arises from the fact that only a varying part of the total exports or imports of any given country is recorded in the statistics ordinarily published. This part is usually called the "visible" trade. What is and what is not visible, however, depends entirely upon the eyes of the viewer. In many cases, official vision is so bad that it fails to note so obvious an item as an ocean liner (or a whole fleet of them) sold to foreign interests. Official statistics, in fact, merely show the results of that portion of foreign commerce which happens to be easy of surveillance, or they reflect the statistical whims of legislatures. They are of no value whatever for most of the purposes to which they are ordinarily applied. Whether, under myopic legislation, trade is or is not "visible" is, from the economic point of view, completely irrelevant. No distinction will be made in this book, therefore, between so-called visible and invisible items.

[7] Temporary deviations may occur as a result of grossly disturbed monetary conditions. This situation cannot persist indefinitely and usually does not last for any considerable period.

mobile goods cannot deviate far from the similar world level. With prices given, however, wages will be high or low proportionate with productivity.

That differing national wage levels have no causal effect on prices is clearly indicated by the amusing mutual fears of Premier Mussolini and ex-President Hoover. Il Duce vehemently asserts that the Italian worker must be protected against imports from the United States produced at low prices by mass methods and with high efficiency. The former American president is equally convinced that the standard of living of American workers must be guarded by import duties against the output of Italian and other industry where low wages are paid. Premier Mussolini is obviously impressed by what he believes to be the general low unit costs in the United States arising from American productive effectiveness, and Mr. Hoover by what *he* believes to be the general low unit costs in Italy issuing out of Italian low wages. Each believes that his own country, without protection, would be completely undersold by the other. They cannot both be right but both can be, and in fact are, wrong.

Neither efficiency nor low wages gives one country any general competitive advantage over another since, in any lengthy period, they must be inversely proportional to each other. High wages in export industries *cannot* be paid unless effectiveness is high, and they cannot be refused if it is.[8] Similarly, low wages are in-

---

[8] Competition among employers will force money wages into line with the money value of the worker's contribution to output. If wages are less than such contribution, profits will be so high as to set up an urgent demand for labor and raise wages, while if they are more, unemployment will persist until a downward adjustment of wages takes place.

evitable if productivity is low. The two factors balance each other in their effect on costs.

Any common export of Italy and of the United States will be produced in both countries at substantially the same money costs per unit and will, of course, sell at the same price in neutral markets regardless of its origin. As regards other commodities, the money costs per unit of output will, for some of them, be lower in the United States than in Italy and, for others, lower in Italy than in the United States. The former commodities, if mobile, will be exports of the United States and, under free trading conditions, imports of Italy. The latter commodities, if mobile, will be exports of Italy, and, under free trading conditions, imports of the United States. Neither the United States, Italy, nor any other country could ever in all lines undersell, or be undersold by, another; but every country, whatever the height of its wage structure, will be able, as long as it permits any imports at all, to undersell other countries in some lines just as it will be undersold by them in others.

Such is the automatic issue of the international price mechanism under free trade, protection, or any other policy. Under *any* policy price levels will undergo such minor shifts relative to one another as are necessary to bring the value of total exports into equilibrium with that of total imports. Any policy which restricts either total exports or total imports will therefore tend to restrict the other in equal degree. Far from the wage structure determining prices, it is prices, together with productive effectiveness in export industries, which determine monetary wage rates. Money wages and other incomes vary with changes in (1) the money factor, and

(2) the productivity factor. The one is, in the long run, of no concern to prosperity; the other is the essence of it. The one has no effect on *real* incomes; the other is vital to them.

Abstraction being momentarily made of the question of employment, it is clear that protective tariffs can have no general effect on maintenance of standards of living. Tariffs, as such, cannot, of course, improve the resources in any country or the skill and diligence with which they are worked, though they can, and usually do, tend to give them a disadvantageous direction. They can scarcely increase the prices at which *exports* are sold or, therefore, the wages in these bellwether industries. If protective tariffs had any general influence in making or keeping a people prosperous there would be no poverty in the world. Standards of living, however, cannot be raised or maintained by legislative fiat nor are they adversely affected by general free competition.

Competition always seems less desirable to the particular competitors involved than does a monopoly. It seems more desirable, however, to everyone else. It is, moreover, usually beneficial to the whole. This is as true of foreign as of domestic competition. Protective import duties give exclusive possession of the domestic market to certain classes of domestic producers but they do so only at the expense of other domestic producers and of consumers who cannot be so sheltered. It is therefore credulous in the extreme to suppose that "protection" can be universal or that it can have any *general* tendency to raise or maintain standards of living. Once the notion is grasped that high real wages, far from deriving from high prices, are on the whole inconsistent with them, confusion on this issue disappears.

THE LAW OF COMPENSATION IN IMPORTS AND EXPORTS

Turning now to the effect, if any, of a liberal trade policy on employment, it should first be noted that, unless a nation is quite peculiarly lucky, it cannot secure imports without paying for them, and that payment for any increase of imports due to a liberal commercial policy cannot finally be effected without giving rise to domestic employment on exports to a value equivalent to that of the expanded volume of goods secured from abroad.[9] Imports will simply not enter a country unless there is an equivalent volume of exports.[10] This would be ob-

---

[9] We frequently hear of the danger of an "inundation" of foreign goods. If such an "inundation" should ever materialize it would be a case of showers of blessings. The question as to who would be so generous as to send this wave of good things to our shores, without securing anything in return, has never been satisfactorily answered. If it could be, the citizens of the "inundated" country could all go fishing, meanwhile living at a high standard on the bounty of foreigners, without even the necessity of catching any fish.

It has, in particular, been alleged that the capitalistic world is in "danger" of such an inundation from Russia. The realization of this "danger" would surely be the triumph of capitalism since it would make the Russians the slaves of the capitalistic world. In fact, the Russians are not so foolish as to export anything except with the conscious aim of thereby securing the means to pay for imports. The Russian dictatorship is brought face to face with the problem of providing as well as possible for its population, and is not unaware of the fact that to secure imports at a lower cost (in exports) than must be paid if such imports were made in Russia is a great contribution toward that end.

The disrupting effects of sudden *changes* in the conditions of international competition cannot, however, be denied. An influx of imports far beyond the usual scale may provoke partial or general unemployment even though payment is effected by the export of commodities, other than gold, from accumulated stocks. This phenomenon is not peculiar to countries of liberal commercial policy and will presently be treated in greater detail.

[10] Abstraction is here made, for the moment, of international borrowing and lending, which will be later discussed.

vious if international commercial transactions were, in form, the barter which they are in fact. But here, as elsewhere in economics, the use of money (or of instruments with certain monetary characteristics) pulls wool over our eyes. The statement erroneously attributed to Lincoln that "when we buy goods abroad we get the goods and the foreigner gets the money whereas when we buy goods at home we have both the goods and the money," seems to the man on the street like inspired common sense. In truth, however, in its implications at any rate, it is arrant nonsense. A domestic trading transaction does not, of course, alter either the amount of goods or the amount of money in the country. A purchase of foreign goods with gold, on the other hand, alters both. It alters them, however, in opposite directions, increasing the amount of goods and diminishing the amount of money. Since the goods would not have been bought if they had not been worth more to the purchaser than the money material which he gives for them, there seems to be no reason for inhibiting the transaction.

It will be worth while, however, to follow somewhat farther the purchase of foreign goods for money. Let us suppose, first, that every foreign commercial transaction involved a cash payment by the importer to the exporter. Since gold is the only thing which even closely approximates an international money we may, for the moment, take such cash to be gold, whether in the form of coin or bullion.[11] There are only two ways for any

---

[11] Silver is used in some countries. It does not seem worth while, however, to include silver in this exposition. The principles are precisely analogous whether gold or silver is used. Bills of exchange are not money and will presently be considered separately. Paper money, whether convertible or inconvertible, has practically no

country to get gold. It may produce it within its own borders or it may secure it from abroad. If it *produces* gold, the provision of the gold by means of which foreign commodities are purchased has obviously given employment to its own miners to an amount which would not have been called for if there had been no import of goods. If, on the other hand, such a country had originally secured the gold abroad it must have paid for it by the export of goods or services.[12] The provision of such goods or services must have given employment to its population.[13] The gold, moreover, can be used again to pay for imports to the country in question only after it has been repossessed, presumably in exchange for exported commodities and services the production of which involves employment.

It will be clear that the situation is essentially the same if, instead of giving gold in exchange for foreign goods, such goods are paid for in the usual way by a bill of exchange, or draft, giving the importer of commodities, on payment of an equivalent in his own money, the command over the requisite amount of foreign currency which he proceeds to assign to the exporter. If we take a normal transaction of this type, involving an American importer as the purchaser from an American bank of a sum of foreign currency, elementary analysis will show that, apart from loans and other financial

---

circulation outside its country of origin and thus does not here come in question.

[12] The acquisition of gold by gift, theft, or other non-commercial method, is ordinarily of such slight quantitative importance as to be safely neglected. It will, in any case, presently appear that such receipts have no probable effect on employment in either country concerned.

[13] The writer is far from supposing that what a country needs is employment rather than products but, in view of popular psychology, it seems best to present the matter in this light.

transactions, the stock of foreign currency from which the sale is made by the bank must derive from an export of gold, other commodities, or services from the United States; that, whichever of these is the source of the exchange, its production for export must have provided employment for American labor; and that the replacement of the amount of foreign exchange taken by the importer (the condition of the continuance by the bank in this business and of sales to later importers) involves further employment at home in the export trades. With whatever variations exchange transactions may be conducted, the result will be the same.

THE EFFECT OF INTERNATIONAL BORROWING AND LENDING

As far, however, as imports are financed with the proceeds of net foreign borrowing or other financial resources, there is no necessity, or indeed possibility, that the total value of the present export of tangible goods or of services will be equal to the total value of such imports.[14] Imports so financed, nevertheless, do not tend to diminish employment in either the borrowing, the lending, or any other, market. A loan by the citizens of one nation to those of another increases the present monetary purchasing power of the borrowers and diminishes that of the lenders. After the loan, the borrowers can buy all that they could have bought in their domestic market without floating the loan, and they can

---

[14] A present bookkeeping equilibrium is attained through the inclusion, *in the account*, of the present worth of a promise of future income, *viz.*, the securities or other rights acquired in exchange for the loan of present purchasing power. For a more thoroughgoing discussion of the balance of payments, see Appendix II.

have the imports as well.[15] The actual borrowers, of course, may sell, for their domestic currency, the foreign exchange proceeds of the foreign loan. The purchasers of this exchange will then take the increased volume of foreign goods for which alone the borrowed money can be spent. In compensation, the original borrowers will extend, in equal measure, their purchases in the domestic market, using in payment the proceeds of their sale of the foreign exchange arising from their borrowing operation. Though a foreign loan cannot ultimately be used except to make purchases in the country of the lender, this in no way, therefore, diminishes the demand for domestic goods on the part of the borrowers or their compatriots.

If now we look at the lending country, we shall find that although, after a foreign loan, the lenders' immediate ability to purchase in their own or any other market is reduced, this reduction in their demand for domestic goods is compensated by the increased demand from abroad which must issue from the borrowers or from those to whom the borrowers assign the proceeds of their loan. Payment of interest, repayment of principal on old loans, and gifts put the payers, or donors, in the same position as lenders, and the receivers in the same position as borrowers, under a new loan. International borrowing and lending, payment and receipt of interest and amortization, as well as donations, tribute, or theft of money, have therefore no bearing on the total monetary demand for the products of *any* of the countries involved.[16] The *direction* of the demand is shifted, but

---

[15] Since they would presumably not borrow if they had other resources, their *ability* to purchase will evidently be exerted to its full extent both before and after the loan is made.

[16] Foreign financial transactions tend to effect *some* alteration in

its total volume, in each and all of the countries concerned, tends to remain unchanged.

As a result of more or less foreign lending, of international interest payments, of repayment of old loans, of international gifts, tribute, or the like, the trade of any given country may become more or less international, and the direction in which demand within that country will be relatively strong or weak will show a shift. There is, however, no reason to expect any significant effect on the total volume of employment. The ratio of commodity imports to exports of a country which is a net borrower, or a recipient of interest or principal repayments, will rise, and the same ratio for a country which is a net lender, or a payer of interest or principal, will fall. But there is no inherent reason for these shifts of the ratio of import to export being reflected in the employment situation. With a given amount of employment the proceeds of loans, or former investments repaid, enable the recipients to increase, and they force the lenders or payers to reduce, their consumption. But it is the volume of *consumption*, and not of production, which alters in one country relative to another. What the lender refrains from consuming is taken by the borrower. So far as a liberal trade policy has any effect on international borrowing and lending it is likely to be on the side of an augmentation. This will tend to increase the total of international trade and will alter the ratio of exports to imports according to varying circumstances. Domestic trade will tend to shift in the opposite direction.

---

the demand as between different commodities and some small change in relative national price levels. These are subtleties into which it would be superfluous to enter here. Relative monetary demand is shifted slightly but the case is substantially as here depicted.

Understanding of the facts above developed reveals the folly of "buy at home" campaigns which are merely an appeal to ignorance, prejudice, and credulity. Since any measure which limits imports tends to reduce the value of exports in an exactly equal degree, it can be laid down with certainty that, whatever the causes and cure of unemployment,[17] imports are neither responsible, nor is their curtailment a remedy, for that dread disease.

IMPORTS AS A LABOR SAVER

It should be recognized, however, that while imports call forth exports to an equivalent *value* it normally takes less labor to produce this value in export lines than it would to produce, at home, the imports which are secured in return. This, indeed, is the great advantage of the process. Foreign trade, in fact, effects an improvement in productive powers of precisely the same character as the invention of superior machinery. Both are labor-saving devices making for unemployment in the sense that, with their use, it is not necessary to employ the same amount of labor to secure a given result. The released labor is then available for the satisfaction of a demand which must otherwise remain a desire only.

The sole means to economic progress is this reduction of employment per unit of output. To lay general restrictions on imports is, therefore, on a par with the destruction of machinery or the policy of ca'canny. It will increase the amount of labor per unit of output and therefore diminish the product of a given amount of work. We could, however, make "work" by digging holes and filling them up again. The important thing,

---

[17] For a suggested cure, *cf*. Frank D. Graham, *The Abolition of Unemployment*, Princeton University Press, Princeton, 1932.

though this is often forgotten, is not work but product; and it should be kept in mind that unemployment is perhaps more likely to appear when costs are raised by artificial means than when freedom is the rule.

That the problem of unemployment is not a problem of lack of tasks to be done, of general overproduction, or of "excessive" imports, but solely of dislocated price relationships, will be evident if we turn again to our early economic structure, consider its development, and contrast it with the present economic regime.[18] Where there was little or no communication between families, self-employment was essential. The greater the population the more work there was to be done. If any individual felt that he would rather be idle than increase his stock of commodities, such unemployment as he could afford was purely voluntary and not due to any difficulty in finding work. The general feeling was that there was far more work than anyone wanted. This was true regardless of the state of economic well-being actually realized. Everyone welcomed any device which would save labor and, after some halting communication with the outside world was eventually established, was only too glad to purchase any commodity at less cost than the making of it would exact.

SPECIALIZATION AND EMPLOYMENT

The system of specialization, and indirect coöperation, came into existence gradually as individuals found that they could get more, by domestic or international

---

[18] The following paragraphs draw heavily, even at times to the extent of verbal repetition, from an article by Edwin Cannan, "The Demand for Labor," *Economic Journal*, Vol. XLII, No. 167, pp. 357 *et seq.*

exchange, than by self-sufficient production. No one was so foolish as to suppose that he had been deprived of employment when he abandoned one of his pursuits in order to concentrate on another. The coöperating circle, moreover, could always be expanded without difficulty. Our forefathers used to say that with every mouth there comes a pair of hands; but we are in more need of being reminded that with every pair of hands there comes a mouth, and a mentality with the desire for a far greater supply of economic goods than it has ever been or is likely to be possible for us, as a whole, to satisfy.

In the pioneer stage, and in the simple communities which early developed therefrom, an increase in population or of production per head never gave rise to the notion that it would be necessary to cut down on the hours of work or to keep some proportion of the population idle and living on the rest. There were always unsatisfied wants—we have not escaped from this condition—and if all the population were not immediately employed the "surplus" workers were distributed, or distributed themselves, among existing occupations so as to keep the total production of the several commodities up to the amount "required" for an increasing population; or, where per capita output was rising, to give the community a little more of each of the products already produced; or, finally, to provide new goods such as the community had not hitherto been able to afford. The power to consume here, as always, was conditioned solely by the amount produced, and the whole population was engaged in such proportions in the various industries as were appropriate to domestic needs on the basis of the existing quantum of productive power.

The development of foreign trade meant the shifting of some workers from the production of commodities for the domestic market, in order to provide a "surplus" of other commodities for foreign markets. This left a "deficit" in the supply of the articles in which production was curtailed by the very act of specialization. The "hole" was filled by imports. Exports, in reducing domestic consumption below the purchasing power provided by production, always *must* leave such a hole. If it is not filled by imports it will not be filled at all. Exports will then simply be given away, to the detriment of the standard of living of the donors. Export industries, in fact, do not arise because there is any general surplus of production but solely because it pays to produce a surplus of certain commodities in order to gain, by the export-import process, a larger command over other articles. There is never any *necessity* of foreign markets for the products of any country. Specialization is simply an improved method of production which, like all improvements in production, increases the power to consume *pari passu* with the power to produce. If production were properly distributed as between the various commodities, all of the goods it is possible to produce could readily be consumed at home. It would not be wise to build up such a structure of production, but it is feasible.

Production carried on by self-sufficient individuals, though inefficient from the point of view of *potential* output, has one great advantage in that it facilitates adjustment to changing demand and to improvements in technique. Involuntary unemployment is alien to its nature. Such unemployment occurs only in a specialized exchange society and as a result of *dislocations* inside the coöperating circle.[19]

---

[19] That unemployment is due to dislocations of equilibrium rather than to deeper causes must be obvious when we reflect that in spite of a steady increase in population, a still larger enhancement of pro-

A cessation or diminution of demand for some particular commodity, the discovery of some improved method of producing it, or its acquisition by import at a low price, may render it impossible for some or all of the persons who had been engaged in producing the article in question to continue to find employment in that line or, at any rate, to continue to find employment at a wage equal to that of their fellows in other branches of industry. Such persons do not go back to the old noncoöperative way of living because the condition of persons inside the coöperating circle has become so obviously superior to that of those outside that no one would willingly try to live in isolation. But transference from one specialized occupation to another is not always easy, and it may be hindered artificially by workers already employed in the industry in which an influx of labor would naturally occur.

Specialization, moreover, involves bargaining, and bargaining is attended by disagreements over the rate at which one class of service is to exchange for another. When nearly all bargains are made in terms of money, and especially when the commodity value of money changes, it often becomes so difficult to effect an agreement between those who have specialized in the task of entrepreneur and those who have specialized in the provision of labor services that unemployment on a large scale develops.

---

duction and of imports, and an occasional relaxation of artificial trade barriers, unemployment has practically ceased whenever the temporary dislocations which cause it have disappeared. The proximate cause of unemployment in a capitalistic society is always such a shift of costs of production relative to selling prices as makes it impossible for entrepreneurs to secure a profit on a volume of output sufficient to employ the whole population. Whatever the causes of such a shift—and they are legion—unemployment can always be successfully attacked by a reversal of this process.

Unemployment, once brought into being, is self-generating. The demand of the unemployed, being necessarily restricted by the fact that they have nothing to offer in exchange for the goods they desire, wipes out part of the market for the product of workers still employed. What had been no more than an equilibrium output of the latter product then becomes excessive. This apparent excess leads to new dismissals and these, reflected throughout industry, give rise to another chain of discharges of workers. The real difficulty, however, is not that there is too much general production but that there is too little. It should never be forgotten that demand for any one product or service can come only from the supply of another and that a diminution in general supply automatically cuts general demand in the same degree.[20] On the other hand, an increase in general supply automatically expands demand in equal measure.

This is as true of imports as of any other form of supply.[21] No one, of course, would deny that the exclusion of imports, by a protective duty or otherwise, will, in the levying country, provide employment in

[20] The supply of any one product in an amount sufficient to make its sale, at an equilibrium price, impossible, should always be corrected by a shift of workers to other lines of output. In a pioneer society such a shift from the production of one to another commodity takes place immediately. In an exchange society, however, the transition is effected only with friction, involving unemployment, which, unless counteracted, is self-aggravating. The cure for unemployment is to put people to work in lines in which supply, however large in the absolute, is *relatively* low.

[21] The individuals or countries which send goods into an import market do not necessarily, or even probably themselves take out an equivalent value of goods, in return. However, they secure command over a certain amount of the importing country's currency. It has already been pointed out that, if they do not themselves use this currency to make purchases in the only market in which it has validity, they sell it to those who will.

those industries hitherto subject to competition from imported supplies. This is obvious. All that happens, however, is that the former foreign exporters of such articles, no longer being able to secure the currency of the levying country, cannot themselves import goods from that country. Nor, on the assumption that they would not themselves wish to do so, can they furnish its exchange to their compatriots, or anyone else, who would like to use it for that purpose. This is not so obvious, but it is equally true.

No one, moreover, would deny that the elimination of an effective protective tariff would injure the industries which it had hitherto been sheltering. But, in so far as the home market was opened to foreign goods, the foreign market of export industries would, for the reasons above given, show an equivalent expansion. Furthermore, the net saving which issues from a liberal commercial policy releases purchasing power for expenditure on increased consumption and thus increases the demand for workers.

The policy of protection or its reverse has *per se*, therefore, no bearing on the problem of unemployment. On the whole, that problem is likely to be neither greater nor less under a permanent policy of high protective tariffs than under permanent low duties or free trade. While there is no virtue in protection as a cure for unemployment, there is also no case against it on this score. Objections to protection must be put on the ground not that it hinders employment but that it diverts employment into relatively unproductive channels. The real question is whether the composition of the national industry, under a policy of protection, is as effective a producing mechanism as the industrial structure which would be built up in its absence. The ultimate test of any commercial policy must be the product which issues under its provisions. Unemployment might conceivably be a factor to be taken into account. It is not in fact, however, of any importance in a consideration of the relative merits of permanent and general high protection and of unrestricted foreign trade.[22]

CHANGES IN COMMERCIAL POLICY AS A FACTOR IN UNEMPLOYMENT

It should be noted, however, that, though the commercial policy of any country, whether it be restrictive or liberal, is in the long run of no relevance to the problem of unemployment, it is nevertheless true that *sudden* changes in policy, especially where unemployment is already great, are likely to increase the existing difficulties. This is true whether the shift is from free trade to protection, protection to free trade, or merely from a lower to a higher, or a higher to a lower, general protective schedule. All involve a dislocation of markets and such dislocations are never unaccompanied by friction. Unemployment, being a problem of maladjustment and friction, is, in consequence, likely to be accentuated by changes in tariffs in *either* direction.

If, when protective tariffs are raised, the displaced

---

[22] The freer the trade the greater will be the degree of specialization and the larger will be the market, for any given product, of any given producing area. It is sometimes argued that a large market makes for stability and, other things being equal, this would seem to be true. On the other hand, a narrower home market is often thought to be more stable than a market which includes both foreign and domestic consumers, and it is certainly less likely to be wiped away in part by foreign legislation in which the producer has no voice. It is not unlikely that specialization might furnish greater stability (less unemployment) in some cases and that self-sufficiency might do so in others. No general rule can be laid down, and the matter is reserved for later discussion.

workers in such export industries as are injured by the change were immediately absorbed by the industries destined to expand under the ægis of the new schedules, or if, when protective tariffs are lowered, the displaced workers in the formerly highly protected import industries were immediately absorbed in the export industries now destined to grow, all would be well. But this does not happen. Moreover, the chances are always strong that for some time the workers displaced under any tariff revision, up or down, will exceed in number those for whom jobs open up.[23]

This does not, of course, mean that tariff policy should never be changed (though frequent, and opposite, changes are a profound nuisance) but that it should not ordinarily be changed for the purpose of coping with unemployment. It is necessary, however, to cite some exceptions. In the first place, it seems not improbable that the latest of our crises, with its accompaniment of huge unemployment, was in some measure due to a conflict between a comparatively free system of international finance and a highly restricted system of international trade. International finance being merely an adjunct to international trade, a complete throttling of international trade would render international finance quite nugatory. The economic world cannot well get along half-slave and half-free.[24] The restraints actually

---

[23] Whether this is or is not so depends to some extent on the general conjuncture. If the change is made on the up-swing of a business cycle all may perhaps go smoothly; if not, things are likely to become worse. It is always possible to discharge workers immediately; but new workers cannot, in large numbers, be taken into an industry favored by any tariff change until equipment has been provided. This takes time.

[24] Either there will be an upward movement of trade more in correspondence with the present volume of international indebted-

imposed on international trade by nearly all nations have been a factor of some importance in tying knots in an international financial system relatively free of political interference.

Financial stress has, in turn, reacted adversely on both foreign and domestic trade and on employment. A scaling down of tariff walls, while introducing some new elements of friction, might therefore release immediately, as it certainly would ultimately, much more trade than it would temporarily embarrass. The general psychological effect of such freedom, moreover, might be so good that, to the probably dominant extent to which depression is due to psychological causes, there would be a marked impetus toward improvement.

The case, however, is rather to be put on the ground that permanent mutual benefits would accrue from a general reduction of absurdly developed "protective" structures than that such reductions would prove temporarily expedient in reducing unemployment. That this is so will be clear when it is recalled that extensions, rather than reductions, of protective duties are frequently advocated as a cure for unemployment and that the argument does not always lack cogency. Unemployment being a problem of maladjustment and dislocation, the disturbing force which, in any situation, has promoted unemployment may sometimes be counteracted by another factor, in itself unsettling, which happens to give a jolt in the opposite direction. According to circumstances the appropriate jolt might be given by the imposition, or increase, of duties quite as well as by their removal or remission.

Protective tariffs were advocated by eminent authori-

ness, or there will be a forced downward adjustment of indebtedness to a restricted volume of trade.

ties in Great Britain in the early post-war period and later, on the ground that they would reduce the real wages of the British worker, would thus counteract the failure to deflate monetary wages to a level which, with due regard for changes in efficiency, would have corresponded with post-war prices and the increase in the gold value of the pound, and would, in consequence, permit the emergence of the profits on which employment depends.[25]

The wisdom of a tariff policy which, in an attempt to cure a present evil better attacked in other ways,

---

[25] Protection was also advocated in Great Britain as a means for improving the "balance of trade," that is, preventing an efflux of gold. It must be conceded that, in certain circumstances, protective tariffs might be efficacious to this end as well as offering some temporary relief from the burden of unemployment. Before their imposition the levying country may be paying for part of its imports by drafts on its normal stock of gold, serving monetary purposes, without a corresponding reduction of the currency supply. The original acquisition of the exported gold must have given employment, and its presumptive repossession would do likewise. For the moment, however, imports are being paid for, in part, in a way which does not immediately stimulate production. This is true in all cases in which a nation lives temporarily on its fat, that is to say, on capital accumulations of some sort or on credit and, while doing so, permits an undue volume of unemployment to persist. The reason for such a development is practically always a domestic price level above the equilibrium position. The appropriate action, long recognized, is a downward adjustment of the price level. The unwillingness to take this action, coupled with a desire to remain on the gold standard, is then used as an argument for protective tariffs, which *might* preserve both the desiderata, but only at the expense of potential real incomes. While a country may temporarily live on its capital or credit and thus for a time consume foreign products in excess of its *current* delivery of a *quid pro quo*, the fact has no direct bearing upon employment or upon commercial policy. The phenomenon might happen with or without full employment and under *any* commercial policy. It is sometimes alleged that an idle *rentier* class is essential to a position in which interest is received on a large net foreign investment. This is nonsense. Neither an individual nor a country need be idle because he happens to be a *rentier*.

would confessedly reduce in perpetuity the potential income of the levying country, is, however, surely open to question. Commercial policy should be based on long- rather than short-term considerations and should not be prostituted to ends which it was never designed to serve. The very idea of policy involves something more than opportunistic adaptation to disorder. Since neither a liberal nor a restrictive commercial policy, *per se*, makes either for or against full employment, their relative merits can be estimated without reference thereto.

The real issue is whether the presumptively equal *volume* of employment which will prevail under either policy will be more or less efficacious in providing the population with the goods it desires. Maximum product per unit of working time (the amount of work undertaken being a matter of choice of the relative satisfactions to be obtained from a larger supply of commodities or larger leisure) is the real goal of economic effort, and the task of commercial policy is to establish the *milieu* in which such maximum product may be attained.

CHAPTER IV

THE ARGUMENT FOR FREE TRADE

INHERENT ADVANTAGES IN SPECIALIZATION

SINCE prosperity is dependent on prices being low relative to wages and other incomes, a sound commercial policy is that which results in low prices at a given wage level or high wages at a given price level.[1] Fundamentally this depends on efficiency in production, but it is also conditioned by the exchange of the produced goods. It is, of course, in the exchange of goods that the incidence of commercial policy is first felt, but it affects production as well. It is the contention of free traders that unrestricted exchange not only results in the maximum satisfaction from a given stock of goods but that it also brings about maximum production and consumption. The argument in support of this contention will be offered in the present chapter.

As far as the exchange of goods *already produced* is concerned, it is clear that every trading transaction tends to lower the price of the affected commodities in the relatively high-priced market *to* which, and to raise them in the relatively low-priced market *from* which, they move. The constant tendency of trade is therefore

---

[1] Wages (including salaries) are quantitatively the most important type of income and, unless it is otherwise clearly implied, will be used henceforth elliptically to cover incomes in general.

toward ironing out price differences. This is of universal benefit. A high price is evidence of relatively urgent unsatisfied desire, and a low price of comparative satiety. To lower a high price means, therefore, that a rather urgent desire has been supplied, while to raise a low price means only that a somewhat unimportant desire must go unfilled. To put restraints on trade is to forego the satisfaction of a more urgent desire for the sake of fulfilling one of lesser significance, and, of course, it deprives the potential seller of the same advantage as it withdraws from the potential buyer.

The question, however, is not only, or even mainly, that of maximizing the satisfactions from a stock of goods already produced, but, more important, of maximizing the volume of goods steadily issuing from farms, mines, and factories into consumption. Trade and specialization go hand in hand. Continuous trade is impossible without specialization and specialization is impossible without trade. Specialization, moreover, is the prime element in efficient production and, therefore, in prosperity. Most advances in productive technique since time began are, in some of their aspects, an increase in specialization.

Such specialization is either (1) occupational, or (2) territorial. Of occupational specialization it is unnecessary to say much in this place. Its advantages are universally recognized. The plumber does not attempt to make his own watch, and the watchmaker would but burn his hands if he should attempt to wipe a joint. Not only is there much specialization by trades, but also *within* a given branch of production specialization has gone far to the advantage of all concerned. The entrepreneur in the automobile industry does not, in any literal sense, build automobiles, and the mechanic in that industry would quickly encounter bankruptcy if he should attempt to make a complete car and market it.

On the contrary, every individual, so far as his course is directed by ordinary economic motives, takes up the specialized job at which he can make most money, and this means, in a freely competitive society, the job in which he can produce the maximum value which his talents permit. By concentrating in the line in which his efficiency is greatest he raises that efficiency, for the *whole* of his effort, from a mere average of those things in which he is relatively good and those in which he is relatively bad, to the level of that work in which he is at his best. What this means to production can be vaguely guessed if one considers how poor he himself must be if, instead of concentrating on a single job, he had to produce, in turn, his own food, clothing, shelter, household supplies, transport, and general accessories of civilization.

Unless, however, occupational concentration is supplemented by specialization of a regional type, only a part of the possible increase in general productivity can be achieved. In any given state of technical knowledge the two fundamental factors in production are labor and natural resources. Occupational specialization tends to maximize the productivity of the labor factor while, in the absence of complete mobility of labor as between regions, regional specialization secures the superior utilization of natural resources.[2]

---

[2] International trade in *commodities* has certain great advantages over perfect mobility of labor. The freest trade in *commodities*, while tending to equate prices, would do little toward equalizing wage rates from one country to another, and would, in any event, raise their absolute level. Perfectly free *migration*, on the other hand, would operate strongly toward equalizing wage rates. The

INTERNATIONAL TRADE AND PRODUCTIVE POWERS

International trade fosters both these types of specialization. The advantages of such regional concentration as issues out of differences in climate and other natural resources are fairly obvious; but there is, in addition, an advantage to be gained through exploiting the marked tendency to develop regional *skills* in certain lines of production and giving to human resources everywhere the opportunity of most advantageous use. International trade is therefore indispensable to the attainment of the best results not only from diverse natural resources but also from labor. As long as lines of comparative competence are pursued, the more trade there is the better for all concerned. Trade, however free, will stop when there is no longer *mutual* gain therein. Trade is itself presumptive proof of its own advantage. To put artificial restrictions on trade, on the other hand, is simply to throw away the advantages of regional along with some of those of occupational specialization, and to make a deliberate choice of inefficient methods of production.

Unless subjected to artificial restraint, trade will spring up whenever price differences of more than the cost of transfer of commodities between two markets appear. Such differences in prices will ordinarily arise only from differences in *relative* costs of production. Absolute (effort or sacrifice) costs of production are, as has already been noted, irrelevant. In a certain country

countries of present high wages would have every reason to resent and prevent this process, since high birth rates in the low-wage countries would mean a general leveling *downward* as population pressed on resources. There is no such general reason for inhibiting the free movement of commodities.

the labor of a typical worker may, in one day, produce one unit of wheat, one unit of cloth, or one unit of gold (= $1.00).[3] The gold price of wheat and of cloth in the markets of that country would then tend to be $1.00 a unit, and wages $1.00 per day.[4] In another more productive country the labor of a typical worker may, in one day, produce 3 similar units of wheat, 3 of cloth, or 3 of gold (= $3.00). The gold price of both wheat and cloth in the markets of this as of the other country would then also tend to be $1.00 per unit, but wages would be $3.00 per day. Since there is no difference in *relative* costs of production, there is no difference in either relative or absolute commodity prices. There is thus no occasion for, or advantage in, trade between the two countries. Territorial specialization here offers no benefits.

But where there are differences in *relative* costs of production of the several commodities, either because it is absolutely easier to produce one group of commodities and more difficult to produce another in the first than in the second country, or because, though it may be absolutely more difficult to produce *any* commodity in the one than in the other, it is possible to produce some commodities more easily than others (pro-

---

[3] The monetary unit indicated is arbitrarily chosen. For the sake of convenience the unit taken is equal to the amount of gold in the (former) American gold dollar.

[4] Capital charges may, for convenience, be subsumed under labor. The supposition would then be that, counting the labor necessary for the production of machinery and the price of "abstinence," the results would be as stated. Similarly "wages" is used elliptically for the returns to factors of production taken as a whole. The outlay of effort will, of course, depend, among other things, on the richness of natural resources, while the relative costs of production of various commodities will depend on the adaptability of the human and material resources to one rather than another type of production.

duction in the alternative country being taken as the standard), price differences will emerge, the occasion for trade will arise, and specialization will tend to develop and will yield benefits in increased income for both countries.

Thus if, in a certain country, the labor of a typical worker will produce in one day 2 units of wheat, 1 unit of cloth, or 1 unit of gold (= $1.00), the price of wheat in that country, in the absence of international trade, will tend to be 50c a unit, the price of cloth $1.00, and wages $1.00 per day. In another more productive country the labor of a typical worker will produce, let us suppose, 3 units of wheat, 6 units of cloth or 3 units of gold (= $3.00). Prices in this country, in the absence of international trade, will then tend to be: wheat $1.00 per unit, cloth 50c, and wages $3.00 per day.

Under these circumstances international trade between the two countries—the one exporting wheat and importing cloth, and the other the contrary—will spring up, specialization will occur, and the separate prices of each of the products will move toward an equality in the two countries, though this will be somewhat modified by costs of transportation.[5] The advantage of such specialization will be clear when we note that the first country, for every unit of cloth it ceases to produce, can produce two units of wheat; and that the second, for every unit of wheat it ceases to produce, can produce two units of cloth.

This does not mean a doubling of total production,

---

[5] The production of gold in both countries will tend to be stimulated by the increase in the production of other commodities and the consequent relatively high value of gold. This augmentation of gold production will tend to continue until the costs of production of gold and of the wheat and cloth for which it will exchange are equal.

since there is no increase in productivity on that part of its own specialty which each country was formerly producing for itself; but it does mean, for the two countries as a whole, four units of both products for every three under self-sufficing regimes. The first country would be willing to give anything up to two units of wheat for one unit of cloth, and the second would be willing to take anything more than one-half a unit of wheat for one of cloth. Disregarding transport costs, trade on any terms between one-half to two units of wheat per unit of cloth, or its correlative, one-half to two units of cloth per unit of wheat, will be advantageous to both.

Transport costs have the effect of reducing the price range within which trade would be advantageous, and they may be so great as to eliminate the possibility thereof. The important point, however, is that whenever prices, including transport, make trade advantageous to one party they automatically make it advantageous to the other. Trade and specialization increase the total output and the income of both parties to the transaction.

Comparative advantage (competence) and disadvantage (incompetence) are, of course, correlative. Regardless of absolute productive powers, the possession by any country of a comparative competence in the production of one commodity is *ipso facto* the possession of a comparative incompetence in the production of another. If, judged by the standard of another country, it is comparatively easy to produce in a certain locale one of two commodities, it must be comparatively difficult to produce the other. Similarly, using the other of two countries alternatively as a standard, any commodity which it is comparatively easy to produce in one country must be comparatively difficult of production in the other. That the former, the less productive of the two countries used above for purposes of illustration, has a comparative competence in the production of wheat inevitably implies not only that it is comparatively incompetent in the production of cloth but also that the latter of the two countries is comparatively incompetent in the production of wheat, along with its comparative competence in the production of cloth and its greater *absolute* competence in the production of both commodities.

The question is not whether any given country is in general, or in a specific commodity, a more effective producer than another, but which of two or more commodities it can produce most effectively. Iceland may not be able to raise either potatoes or peaches without great difficulty; but if, judged by the situation in other countries, it can, value for value, raise potatoes more easily than peaches the Icelanders would be foolish not to concentrate on the tuber. It would be equally foolish for the United States to exclude imports of potatoes from Iceland and thus lose a market for its peaches as compared with which potatoes can be produced in the United States only at a disadvantage.[6] The United States price for peaches will be low and the price for potatoes high, as compared with Iceland, which means, of course, that the contrary will be true of Iceland as compared with the United States.

Whatever complications may be introduced by the injection of additional countries and additional commodi-

---

[6] Potatoes must, of course, be grown in the United States since Iceland could supply only a part of the American demand. However, so far as trade with Iceland reduces American production of potatoes and increases its production of peaches, the United States will share in the benefits of the trade. The potato lands in the United States *least* fit for that crop, relative to an additional output of peaches for the new market, will be turned over to peach growing.

ties, it will remain true in any situation that specialization along lines of the greatest comparative competence or, what is the same thing, the least incompetence, will increase total output; that this increase in output will be shared more or less equally among the trading groups; and that free trading conditions will, through the play of prices, promote this specialization. Production of any one commodity involves the loss of opportunity to produce, with the same human and material resources, some other good, and free trade leads to the best selection of opportunities.

UNIVERSAL CHARACTER OF THE FREE TRADE ARGUMENT

This is the universally valid analysis underlying the argument for free trade. Time, place, and circumstance are irrelevant thereto. Whether a country is rich or poor, big or little, new or old, with or without high standards of living, agricultural, industrial, or mixed, makes no difference. It is a matter of mathematics, quite independent of environment, that there is an *inherent* gain in the specialization along the lines of *comparative* competence which unshackled trade tends to develop.

There is no possible refutation of this analysis. Advocates of a restrictive commercial policy must, in logic, accept it as a fact and attempt to show that the gain may be outweighed by economic or other considerations of superior importance. Their case must rest not on proximate but on ulterior considerations such as those to which attention is drawn in the following chapter. The *presumption* is always in favor of free trade, since the gain therefrom is certain, and the loss, if any, dependent upon incidental circumstance. This presumption is rebuttable but it is ever present; and, in this sense, the classical economists were right in insisting that free trade is a ubiquitous and timeless principle. Other things being equal, it will enable people to have more goods of every kind than would otherwise be possible.[7]

This universal argument may be supplemented by noting that collateral in addition to direct, benefits are not precluded under a liberal commercial regime and that, over and above its *inherent* advantages, the chance of incidental gains[8] is at least as good under free trade as under any system of protection not specially chosen to secure such gains. With no change whatever in general skill or resources, there will be an increase in total output arising from the superior form of their utilization which will occur under free trade. This is the inherent gain. But it is by no means improbable that the specialized character of such production will have favorable collateral effects which may even greatly surpass in quantitative importance those which are inherently present. This is obvious in the case of occupational specialization where increased practice leads to greater skill, involves no waste of time in shifting from one occupation to another, and makes possible a more intensive use of machinery.[9]

---

[7] This is the true test of economic soundness. Any process which creates the potentiality of securing, at a given cost, a larger volume of *every* economic good is economic, and its converse uneconomic. Whether the population concerned actually elects to take more of *every* good, or more of some and not of others, or prefers additional leisure to more goods, is irrelevant.

[8] Inherent benefits are such as are *bound* to occur. There may be a greater or less assurance with respect to incidental benefits but they do not amount to a certainty.

[9] Specialization enables a worker to use a single machine continuously, whereas in diversified production a large part of the equipment of the worker is necessarily idle most of the time. With a given technique the volume of machinery per unit of output must

It is equally true of regional specialization. In a district in which a single industry is concentrated the population tends to develop a peculiar skill in that industry. This is probably because children are reared from infancy in familiarity with its ways and instruments and so acquire an ability which others cannot match. There are other gains. The congregation in any locality of a large number of plants of any single industry leads to increases in productivity arising from (1) the rapid diffusion of improved methods, (2) inventions stimulated by intimate association and rivalry, (3) the concentration of ancillary industries in the same neighborhood, (4) the lowering of freight costs, and (5) the lowering of costs of labor turnover. Many of these advantages are of course obtained, in lesser or greater degree, in such protectionist countries as themselves embody a great free trade area. The freer the trade, however, the more probable is their extension.

The improvement of technique is not only furthered by the local concentration of industry but is likely to proceed much more rapidly under the stimulus of free foreign as well as domestic competition than would otherwise be the case. It is no unusual thing for producers of a protected product which, as a result of improved processes introduced abroad, is suddenly subjected to keen competition from foreign sources, to clamor for an increase in tariffs rather than adopt or improve upon the best methods currently in use. Free trade will kill such industries as, from the national point of view, represent wasted productive power, but it will provide a needed stimulus not only for industries of present comparative competence but also for such others

therefore be much greater without, than with, occupational specialization. This involves a needless waste of effort and resources.

as are well fitted for survival, but, at the moment, are stagnating under shelter of the state. The state is economically only as strong as its industry in general, and it cannot cherish a laggard without subtracting from the deserved sustenance of those which are up and doing.

Laissez-faire is by no means a sacred principle. It is to be judged solely on its merits and by its results. Where it leads to monopoly or *mutually* destructive competition it should be abandoned for regulation. In international trade, however, there is far less likelihood of the development of either of these phenomena than in domestic commerce. The case for freedom of international trade is therefore much stronger than that for wholly unregulated internal commercial traffic.

The argument for free trade can perhaps best be put by an analogy with its apparent opposite. If a benevolent and prescient dictator should set himself the task of devising the commercial policy which would best serve the economic interests of his people, he would not limit imports or go in for national self-sufficiency. Whether the natural resources under his control were good or bad, and whether the population he was directing was skillful and industrious or inept and lazy, they would be better adapted to the production of some than of other commodities. With self-sufficiency, the national standard of living could not but be lower than it would be if part of the home production of such goods as the country was best fitted to produce were exchanged against foreign goods. The dictator would receive imports gladly, as long as they were cheap, in the sure knowledge that they would enhance the economic welfare of his people. The productive effort saved in the provision of the relatively small volume of home output which need' be exported in payment for each unit of imports could then be turned toward supplying the domestic market with goods which it must otherwise forego. The margin at which import should cease would be that at which the cost of an imported commodity would be no less than if it were made at home. In a word, the dictator would follow a policy of free trade regardless of the status of wealth and income which his people had, at any moment, attained. The greatest wisdom might well find no opportunity in a direction of trade other than along the lines which the untrammeled action of individuals would tend to give it.

ACHILLES' HEEL

At an earlier point it was stated that, *other things being equal*, free trade will enable people to have more goods of every kind than would otherwise be possible. It is toward this phrase, *other things being equal*, the Achilles' heel of the argument, that protectionists must direct their fire. Is the situation which evolves under free trade conditions devoid of objection? Granting the inherent advantages of *laissez-faire* in commercial policy, are the incidental effects in any given situation desirable? Conceding the direct loss in restrictive measures, what of future indirect results? Accepting the probability of evil consequences from *thoroughgoing* protection, is it not well to shape the structure of national industry toward certain conscious ends not realizable without governmental interference? It is to questions of this sort that attention must now be turned.

CHAPTER V

RATIONAL PROTECTION

THE fundamental free trade argument is potent but not necessarily conclusive. It may be taken for granted that the proximate effects of unrestricted commerce are good, and that there is no *general* reason for supposing that the ulterior effects may not also be desirable. On this latter point, however, there is nothing like a certainty of beneficence. It may be that, in given circumstances, an induced deviation of production and trade from its *laissez-faire* channels will yield otherwise unattainable ulterior benefits more than sufficient to balance the present and future direct losses arising from a policy of restriction. Such benefits may be absolute or they may be national only, that is to say, correlated with more than compensatory losses to nations other than that which imposes the restrictions.

Since protection is essentially a *national* policy it must, perhaps, be held to have been successfully applied whenever a gain accrues to the levying country, whether or not such gain is at the greater expense of other nations. This is, of course, to grant without contention the postulates of nationalism, and it should be pointed out that gains attained by one nation at a more than proportionate cost to others are likely to be nullified by counter activities on the part of the outside world. The result is a net loss all around. Far stronger therefore are those arguments for protection which center around a rational estimate of the probability of absolute unalloyed gains.

The case for protection is sometimes put upon a wholly non-economic basis, with production and trade led into channels adverse to productivity for ends which are deemed superior to national opulence. Such ends are indefinitely numerous, subject to few or no scientific criteria, and emotional rather than rational in content, with their validity therefore impossible of measurement. Only the more widely current of the non-economic arguments will, in consequence, be noted in this chapter. It is probable, however, that nothing of major importance will thereby be omitted.

THE ATTACK ON SPECIALIZATION

The most sweeping rejection of the free trade thesis is associated with scepticism toward specialization as such. Since specialization is the sole medium through which the asserted economic advantages of free trade accrue, an attack on the principle of specialization clearly involves a shrewd thrust at the very heart of free trade doctrine. The pleas for protection based on the allegation of virtue in a diversification of the national economic structure carry farther, therefore, than any of the numerous special arguments which may be brought in support of a restrictive policy.

Diversification of the national economic structure may be advocated on the following grounds:

(1) *Development of Latent Talent.*—If, in any given nation, free trade would promote specialization in a highly restricted group of industries it might have a repressive effect upon progress. If, for example, comparative competence, in a certain nation and at a certain period, lies in agricultural rather than manufacturing pursuits it might well happen, under free trade, that there would be much mechanical talent, and perhaps inventive genius, which would never find an opportunity to express itself. The nation and the world would be the poorer for its suppression. This argument was used by the original sponsors of protection in this country, was greatly developed by Frederick List, and, in certain circumstances, is cogent. It is possible, moreover, that national specialization in mechanical pursuits might smother latent genius in botanical or zoölogical activities just as specialization in the latter occupations may lead to a waste of mechanical genius.

(2) *Insurance.*—Dispersion of risk is, of course, a fundamental principle of insurance, and diversification of industry disperses the national risk from vicissitudes peculiar to single industries or groups of industries. The value of insurance depends, of course, upon its cost relative to the risks against which safeguards are feasible. The risks arising from a specialization of the national economic structure are perhaps increasing as the ratio of the value of fixed capital to annual output rises, and the cost of suddenly effecting a considerable alteration in the character of the national production is thereby enhanced. The argument from insurance is probably, therefore, of growing importance. As economic life has developed in capitalistic countries, there are two separate dangers in high specialization in agri-

cultural and in manufacturing industry respectively. A country fully specialized in agriculture is subject to great vicissitudes in the ratio at which it exchanges its exports for its imports since the prices of agricultural commodities commonly fluctuate, through a business cycle as well as over shorter periods, much more widely than do those of manufactured goods. When the movement is downward such a country may suffer acute distress. A country, on the other hand, fully specialized in manufacturing industry, though benefiting by a change in the terms of trade adverse to agricultural nations, is likely at such times to experience severe unemployment. There is, in consequence, something to be said for a balanced economy in which the fluctuating tendency of the prices of agricultural commodities is compensated by comparative stability in the prices of manufactured goods, while the pains of unemployment in manufacturing industry are alleviated by the comparative steadiness of activity on the farms.

Protection, at a more or less definite price in total productivity, may not only be used to secure such a balanced economy but, in certain favorable circumstances, protective duties may be so manipulated as in some measure to prevent disequilibrizing fluctuations in the relative prices of agricultural and manufactured commodities and the unemployment which issues therefrom.[1] The long-run result may be a net gain in *actual*

---

[1] Such a country as France, for instance, in which important types of agricultural production are ordinarily somewhat, but not greatly, short of domestic consumption, may, by manipulation of protective duties, keep the internal prices of such production comparatively stable and so exert a steadying influence on the national industry in general. An economic structure of this special type, however, inevitably implies a counter structure in other countries. It cannot be generalized and it probably imposes greater instability on other

national production even though productive *potentiali-ties* are reduced.

While the "latent talent" and "insurance" pleas for protection are perhaps the only rational grounds for objection to specialization *as such,* certain *types* of specialization may, on other grounds, be held to be less desirable than diversification. Some forms of concentration of industry may inhibit the growth of an eventually superior specialization of a different and more complex character. If, in given circumstances, the former type would develop under free trade, a case may be made for protection as appropriate to that time and place. There is in almost every agricultural country a strong sentiment in favor of a modicum of protection to manufacturing industry on the ground that, in the long run, manufactures make for prosperity. This is, in large part no doubt, an illusion (certainly some almost purely agricultural countries are in the van of prosperity), but there are reasons for believing that it is not wholly so. There are economic activities which are dependent upon a social environment in which population is locally concentrated. The fairly even dispersion of population which specialization in agriculture tends to produce may therefore fail to secure advantages which would more than compensate the proximate loss involved in discriminatory measures designed to foster manufacturing industry.

Manufacturing pursuits tend to distribute population in fish-net fashion along well-developed lines of traffic with a concentration at certain nodal points. Such a demographic structure greatly lowers the unit cost of

countries than would otherwise obtain. National diversification of production *as such,* however, may be universally applied and, unfortunately, is in fact practiced with excess of enthusiasm.

many commodities such as piped water, gas, gasoline, oil, and electricity; while all economic benefits associated with communication, among which may be listed education (including library facilities), social amusements (theater, opera, concerts, movies), postal, telegraph, and (within limits) telephone service, road and rail transport, news and information, can then be provided at indefinitely lower per capita outlay.

The cost of retailing more tangible commodities is also lowered by a local concentration of population, particularly in goods other than the most common staples. Volume of sales is the most important factor in diminishing the cost of distribution of such articles and a large volume is not attainable in the general store so typical of an agricultural environment. Division of labor is limited by the extent of the market, and a large market for any one purveyor often depends upon a concentration of population. A given specialization is sometimes, therefore, the enemy of a much more thoroughgoing division of labor—the good may be inimical to the better. A restrictive policy which curbs concentration in pursuits which scatter population may therefore, with fruitful economic results, release a much greater volume of specialization than it suppresses.

Taking all these factors into account, and not coming too near to our own times for an illustration, it seems not unlikely that the growth in the prosperity of the northern relative to that of even the white population of the southern states, in our national though not in our colonial history, was due in some measure to environmental factors conditional upon the development of manufacturing industry in the North. The South was of course bled by the national policy of protection to manufactures, and part of the prosperity it would otherwise have enjoyed was drained off to the North.[2] This, however, would merely have tended to equalize conditions between the naturally more favored South and the bleaker parts of the Union; it does not account for the differential in *favor* of the northern section. Greater productive and business energy may be alleged as a cause of the more rapid advance of the Yankee states, but it must remain a question whether this energy was not an effect rather than a cause of dynamic environmental influences.

There are limits, of course, to the economic benefits to which concentration of population gives rise. Extreme density of such concentration makes transport more expensive rather than cheaper, good housing becomes more difficult to provide, and the *per capita* cost of even some services of communication tends to rise. Rising unit costs of production are, indeed, the underlying general tendency of an increase of population in a given area. This is the well-known "law of diminishing returns."

But this general tendency may, at any given stage, be more than offset by counter influences. Any increase in population on a given area, *under a given industrial structure*, is likely, indeed, to be attended by higher unit costs of output. Such increase, however, may itself induce such changes in the industrial structure as will lower those costs. Moreover, the argument above made turns on the *form of distribution* of a given population rather than on total numbers. A rise in the total numbers in a given area will provide some of the advantages due to clustering, but clustering will occur under certain forms of industry and not under others,

---

[2] The deleterious effect of the Civil War upon the South is obvious. The contrast is more effective if only the pre-Civil War period is considered.

however sparse the average density of settlement may be.[3]

OBJECTIONS TO SPECIALIZATION IN SPECIFIC INDUSTRIES

Protection as a means of nullifying allegedly undesirable specialization may be directed not only against a given *type* of economic development but also against what is held to be an undue extension of specific industries. The positive aspect of this argument is for such diversification as will result from the nurturing of industries felt to be specially desirable. The principal economic, or socio-economic, grounds for such negative or positive protection are:

(1) *Conservation of Natural Resources.*—It is usual for a country to possess comparative competence in the production of commodities for which it has great natural advantages. There is an immediate gain in developing international trade along these lines, but the gain arises in part because valuable and irreplaceable natural resources are presented to such a nation, by nature, free of cost. It may well happen that under these conditions products will be offered to foreign countries at prices which at a later time will seem to have been ridiculously

---

[3] Transport is also a factor of great importance. Railroads may often justify the expenditure made upon them though, in the beginning, they were uneconomic. Similarly the establishment, by subsidy, of an ocean transport line, in lieu of service by casual tramp steamers, may prove to have been well-advised in spite of initial experience to the contrary. Since protection by tariffs is ordinarily not feasible in the shipping industry resort is had to subsidies. Direct subsidies have, in general, many advantages over the indirect bounty involved in protective duties. One of their real advantages, however, the fact that they do not conceal the truth, accounts for their decline in political favor, and they are now so little used as not to warrant treatment in this book.

low. This is to sell the national birthright for a mess of pottage. For a small gain now, represented by the difference between the volume of imported products obtained in exchange for the export of the natural resource in question and that of the imported goods which could be produced with the labor and capital devoted to producing the export, such a country foregoes the possibility of a much larger gain later on, whether in a regulated export of the natural resource or in the use of it at home.

To take a concrete instance, we probably are getting a much lower price for oil, and therefore a much smaller physical volume of imported goods for our oil exports, than we could get some years in the future. It would therefore, perhaps, be a wise policy to cut down on our exports of oil. An ordinary protective policy could not of course be very effective here since protective duties ordinarily apply only to imports. By applying duties against imports we cut down on exports *somewhere*, but there is no guarantee that this will greatly curtail the export of any particular product. Aside from direct regulation of production, an export duty would seem to be the only feasible scheme for preventing exports of any given product in which we happen to have a comparative advantage. Export duties, however, are unconstitutional in the United States. There is therefore but slight possibility of supporting conservation by a protectionist policy in the United States, and more direct measures are desirable in any case.

It should be noted, too, that the argument does not apply to replaceable natural resources such as timber so long as prices are fixed in competition with those for planted timber. The supply of the latter timber can be increased at no great increase in cost, and the natural timber might as well be exploited as soon and as quickly as a free movement of trade would occasion. This is said without prejudice to other arguments for conservation of timber, such as prevention of floods and soil erosion.

About the only irreplaceable natural resources are the products of mines, and the prospect of the exhaustion of some of these is too remote to be of much importance. The probability of exhaustion seems to be greater in oil than anywhere else, though iron ore and coal resources are not as good as they used to be and some of the less widely used metals, such as lead, are perhaps in danger of being used up. There is, however, always the possibility that a conservation policy will overreach itself in conserving things which scientific developments make comparatively useless either because better substitutes are found or other ways of producing the conserved resource are discovered. All of these considerations make the possibilities of protection as a support for conservation extremely limited.

(2) *Amelioration of Human Resources.* Comparative competence in a given employment is sometimes due to the presence of a relatively low grade of labor which shows a special bent for the employment in question. A *laissez-faire* policy may result in so great an extension of this employment as, over a period of years or decades, to exert a marked adverse effect on the average quality of the population. The extension of cotton growing in the United States, for instance, was not only originally dependent upon the presence of Negro labor, which we may perhaps not unjustly assume was of lower average quality than the white population, but it also seems to have tended to increase the ratio

of the Negro to the white element in our racial structure. A rather casual examination of population statistics goes to show that, in those states of the Black Belt in which over a period of decades cotton growing has been waxing, the ratio of the Negro to the white population has shown an upward trend relative to those southern states in which cotton culture has been waning.[4] In other words, the demand for a certain type of labor has elicited the supply.

It may be that migration from one state to another has been solely responsible for the shifting ratios but, on the other hand, the shifting may well be due to alterations in the relative birth rates among Negro and white folk in the typically cotton and in the other southeastern states. Had a *laissez-faire* commercial policy been pursued in the United States during the whole of the nineteenth century it would, no doubt, have enlarged the relative importance of cotton growing in our economic life. The possibly consequent higher ratio of Negro to white population would, from the point of view of most whites at any rate, have been undesirable, and would seemingly have lowered the national per capita productive capacity.

If, in the long run, through adjustment of birth rates to relative economic opportunity, the quality of a population tends to adapt itself to the demands which the national industry makes upon it, one might go on to an argument for protection for *any* comparatively incompetent industry provided it could be shown that it would set up a demand for, and possibly evoke a supply of, a larger proportion of high-grade workers than the

---

[4] Other factors, of course, may have been dominant. A much more rigorous investigation of the data would be necessary to assure confidence in the conclusions.

employments it would, as a result of the protective policy, tend partially to displace. Put thus, the argument becomes rather far-fetched. The case, indeed, is seldom clear enough to permit the degree of assurance on which discriminatory legislative action should alone be taken. There is ordinarily no strong reason for favoring one industry rather than another. History does show, however, some instances in which the artificial encouragement of trades requiring highly skilled workers and technicians seems to have had beneficial effects on the character both of the population and of the industry of the country concerned. The argument for protection can be developed, according to circumstances, either toward the diminishing of the ratio of relatively undesired, or toward the increase of relatively desired, elements in the population. In still other circumstances the same objective would call for the abandonment of existing protection.

NURTURING PROTECTION

The historical instances which go to show advantages from the artificial stimulation of certain industries merge into general "nurturing" protection, the fostering of industries during infancy. The infant industry argument for protection, the most popular of the rational pleas for that policy, is, in one aspect, a variant of the thesis on the stimulation of latent and otherwise wasted talent. The infant industry argument, however, goes farther than this, though with decreasing force. It sometimes happens that it is merely the possession of the *incidental* advantages of a particular type of specialization (such as acquired skills) which gives the producers in a given country a continuing comparative competence in any designated product or group of products.

There is, moreover, always an inertia to be overcome in the establishment of new industries and frequently heavy costs of initiation. A stimulus to the assumption of risk may therefore be in order; and the effort to establish, by protection, industries already strongly intrenched abroad may be justified in any given country on the ground that once they have gotten a start they will themselves secure incidental economies which will enable them to produce at prices which will be less than the sum of the prices then prevailing in the standard location, together with costs of transport. This is always a matter of judgment and the limitations on the opportunity for such protection should steadily be borne in mind. These limitations may be summed up as follows:

(1) The infant industry argument hardly ever applies to the protection of agriculture and only somewhat less rarely to any type of extractive industry. This is because: (a) agriculture is chronologically a primary industry in every country and is therefore at any moment as fully developed technically as general conditions permit; (b) agriculture is an industry peculiarly susceptible to increasing costs as production is expanded; and (c) little capital is, as a rule, necessary to start production of most agricultural commodities. Initial difficulties are, in consequence, at a minimum, and no decline in unit costs is to be expected through increase in output. With other extractive industries, such as some types of mining, the initial difficulties are greater. The argument for nurturing protection may therefore be stronger for these industries than for agriculture.

(2) Infant industry protection should be experi-

mental. Whether it is valid or not can be determined in a few years. If the industry continues to "need" protection, this is conclusive evidence that it would have been better never to have granted it. It should be withdrawn gradually, but unflinchingly. It is better that such industries should decline since, under protection, they will block the progress of a better industry. If, after a few years, any protected industry no longer needs shelter, it has justified itself, and whether the statutes giving protection are or are not maintained is a matter of indifference. They are as inoperative in the one case as in the other.

(3) Infant industry protection should not even be contemplated unless it can be shown not only that the industry concerned is likely to be as well carried on as a similar industry in competing countries but that it can be expected to prove technically as competent as is export industry in general in the country levying the duty. To make the whole process worth while the immediate loss must be compensated by an ultimate gain, and this can be attained only when the money cost per unit of output at home becomes less than the price at which such a unit could be imported.

(4) The infant industry argument is becoming less and less applicable as time goes on. In the last century the rapid improvement in productive powers issuing out of the inventions of the Industrial Revolution led to a relatively large development of manufacturing industry since elasticity of demand is much greater along this line than along the line of food-stuff consumption. The protection of manufacturing industry in many countries therefore effected merely an anticipation of what would, in any case, have occurred later. In spite of improvement in agricultural methods, the product *per acre* has

not been greatly increased. The increase in the industrial and urban population of the world has therefore been accompanied by the opening of new lands for the production of food-stuffs. There must be a limit to this process, and the price of agricultural products is therefore likely, in the long run, to rise relatively to the price of manufactures. This means that the chance of establishing profitable manufacturing industry in a non-industrial country is likely to become smaller. There can be no large-scale *substitution* of manufacturing for agricultural production in any country when it cannot transfer to new and sparsely peopled lands the provision of its food supplies.

(5) The infant industry argument is more applicable to a large than to a small country. No export market is immediately open to such an industry. If it were there would be no object in protection. Most of the advantages which the infant industry can hope to secure are advantages attending a large scale of operations. Unless the home market is sizable these are not likely to be obtained. It is quite possible, of course, that the individual plants in a little country should be big; but with industry organized in huge units, as is now the tendency, a small market is a handicap which is often decisive. It is doubtful, for instance, whether the motion picture industry could, through protection, be fostered in a small country, and the same is to some extent true of the automobile and other industries where huge plants dominate the situation.

While, therefore, the infant industry argument is valid in some cases, its scope is much more restricted than is commonly supposed. In the United States a number of important industries (*e.g.*, cotton and silk textiles, iron and steel) have grown, under high protective tariffs, to economic competence, that is to say, they have now reached the stage where they can compete on even, or better than even, terms in world markets. They thus support the case for the nourishing of infant industries. Later important industries, however, such as the automobile, movie, and radio industries, have developed to a huge size with little or no real protection, and they entered foreign markets almost from the beginning. This goes to show that nurturing protection is no longer needed for the development, in this country, of any manufacturing industry economically appropriate to American conditions, and that any such industry which fails to develop spontaneously is unlikely, through protection, to involve other than a waste of the national resources of labor and capital.

The infant industry argument, properly understood, is a mere modification of the idea of free trade. The intelligent advocate of nurturing protection proposes that his measures be but temporary, and he looks forward to the removal at no very distant date of the protection he currently advocates.

In addition to the argument for the protection of infant industry, an argument may in certain circumstances be made for the protection of infant finance. It is conceivable that the lack of a comparative competence in certain lines may be due to a scarcity of capital[5] and that protection of certain industries will promote the growth of capital. This argument, though valid, must be received with caution. The immediate effect of protection must be to diminish income, the source from which capi-

---

[5] Foreign investment may be inhibited by fear, ignorance, or any other of those obstacles to mobility which is assumed in the theory of foreign trade.

tal is derived; and, other things being equal, the accumulation of capital will in these circumstances be checked.

But here again other things may perhaps not be equal. Economic history would seem to show that of two countries with a given income, the one agricultural and the other industrial, the industrial country tends to accumulate capital more rapidly than the agricultural country. Capital is embodied in instruments of production, machinery, buildings, and the like. The very process of growth of manufacturing industry therefore involves the accumulation of capital. Agriculture, on the whole, calls for less capital per unit of product than does most manufacturing industry,[6] and the advantage of capitalistic methods of production is not so great in agriculture as in manufacturing.[7] As a result, a farming community may tend to consume immediately a larger share of its income than an industrial community and so to postpone an improvement in its condition. If this is true, such protection as has the effect of turning production from agriculture to manufacturing industry may, as time goes on, compensate in part or in whole for the immediate loss involved through the stimulus it gives to the accumulation of a larger stock of capital and thus to the improvement of general productive power.

This argument applies of course only to an agricultural country. It would clearly be useless, on this ground, artificially to divert productive power from one

---

[6] Land is here excluded from the concept of capital.

[7] In many types of manufacture a plant must expand or perish. This is usually not true of agricultural productive units. Expansion calls for capital which, under the corporate form of organization now typical of manufacturing industry, is often provided by the corporation itself out of profits. The owners of the corporation are thus led into a quasi-forced saving which does not apply to agricultural entrepreneurs.

manufacturing industry to another, and worse than use-less to divert it from manufacturing to agricultural in-dustry. Further, the more countries which, for this or any other reason, artificially promote industrial develop-ment, the better it is for the countries that do not. The inevitable correlative of an induced development of manufactures in general is the tendency toward increased import or diminished export of non-manufactured articles. The greater the number of countries which indulge in the one type of specialization the stronger, therefore, is the demand for, relative to the supply of, the goods of those countries that remain in the other. This means that more manufactured goods must be offered for a unit of raw materials or food-stuffs. The resulting gain to the countries of extractive industry would quickly wipe away any possible future loss in pro-ductivity issuing out of the failure to accumulate capital as rapidly as might otherwise be done. Artificially fos-tered industrial development involves, therefore, a cer-tain immediate loss for the sake of a very problematical future gain which will surely fail of realization if too many countries go angling for it.

INCREASING VS. DECREASING COST INDUSTRIES

A liberal commercial policy may lead to specialization in industries in which unit cost rises as output is ex-panded, at the expense of industries in which the counter tendency is operative for the time being. So far, at least, as present or prospective economies are external to any given industry it might, at any moment, pay entrepre-neurs to extend their operations in industries of rising unit cost rather than continue in those in which the net tendency of unit costs is downward. As the preceding production of the latter products shrank and unit costs therefore rose, comparative incompetence in such industries would tend to become progressively greater. Though the industries the extension of which is accompanied by rising unit costs should thus constantly offer better returns than are obtainable in other employments, the country might steadily be losing opportunities to improve its *per capita* general productivity and might even suffer an absolute decline therein. Protection for comparatively incompetent industries of declining cost per unit of output might then be warranted.

The argument just given resembles the infant industry plea, with the significant difference that it is not dependent upon the ultimate acquisition of comparative competence in the protected industries. The infant may never grow up but may still be worth cherishing. In its broader aspects, however, the argument merges into that which turns on an economically favorable environment issuing out of the development of a special type of demographic and industrial structure.

The general principle on which all such arguments are based is that of lower unit entrepreneurial or social costs as the scale of output in a given *milieu* is expanded. The lower unit costs may be directly reflected in the output of any given commodity or they may be spread over a wide range of economic goods. The case of joint, or rather common, costs also has a bearing on this issue. Transport, along with production, costs will furnish an example. Most goods, in addition to the cost of production at the point of origin, are subject to transport costs before they come into the hands of the consumer. Rail transport requires a large initial outlay, and large more or less fixed charges are currently incurred regardless of volume of traffic. Under certain conditions a protective policy might increase the traffic on a given railroad system, thereby lower unit costs on all goods transported on the said railroad, and thus more than compensate the immediate loss from protection.

PROTECTION AS A MEANS OF IMPROVING THE TERMS OF TRADE

National benefit, at the greater expense of the outside world, may possibly accrue to any country levying protection, by means of a change in the terms on which its foreign trade is conducted. These terms are best expressed in the relative prices of import and export commodities. From the national point of view the great economic desideratum is to sell the national exports at as high, and to buy the national imports at as low, prices as possible. By protective import duties the national production is shifted in greater or lesser degree from products formerly exported to those formerly imported. An early consequence of this shift is a decrease in the world supply, relative to demand, of the exports of the country which levies the protective duties and an increase in the world supply, relative to demand, of its former imports. The result is a rising tendency in the prices of its exports relative to those of its imports.

The increased national benefit accruing on the foreign trade which such country still carries on will reimburse that country in some measure for the net loss on total production issuing out of the duties. It is conceivable that the shift in the terms of trade might transfer to the country levying the protection so greatly increased a share of the reduced total production of the trading countries as to more than cover the said country's share in the decline in total output. This is the less unlikely to occur when protective duties are imposed upon goods which, under the original conditions, could be produced domestically at a price but little above that at which they could be imported.

The advantage so gained might be permanent. This would occur if, in spite of the change in relative prices, foreign countries should still find it advantageous to continue production much as before rather than shift to those goods which had shown a relative price increase. In fact, however, even a slight temporary rise in the prices of one class of goods relative to those of another class, no alteration having occurred in costs of production, is practically certain to result in relative expansion of the world output of the former and relative contraction of the world output of the latter, and therefore to an ultimate price relationship almost the same as had originally prevailed.

The possibility of snatching a trading advantage by protectionist measures is, in consequence, very slim; and it should further be remembered that, in so far as it is feasible, it is a game at which any number of nations can play. If A gets a trading advantage through the levy of import duties, B, C, and D will probably, through similar measures, be able to shift the terms of trade, in the opposite direction, toward or beyond their original status. The world would then be presented with the sorry spectacle of a competitive exclusion of imports, with the consequent fall in exports[8] and the reduction of total productivity. The scramble for national gain would issue in mutual frustration and reciprocal loss.

---

[8] Even if the interrelationship of the exports and imports of any given country were denied, it is clear that exports and imports, in general, are tied together since the exports of any one country are the imports of others.

NON-ECONOMIC ARGUMENTS

Admitting the economic loss involved in protection, the proponents of that policy often urge that the state is interested in the ethical, biological, sociological, or other welfare of its citizens and that such welfare is often best promoted in ways which involve a present economic loss. They are therefore ready to accept the loss as part of the cost of building up a society more in accord with their ideal.

One group of such arguments is usually brought in support of protection to agriculture on the ground that urbanization is an evil in itself and that the farmer is the "backbone" of the nation. An economist is not specially competent to discuss these matters, but the assumption that rural activities are superior to those of the city as creators of character cannot be said to be proven. There may, however, be some far-off economic reason for viewing with concern a rapid growth of population in a restricted area as a result of specialization in manufacture. As the less crowded parts of the earth fill up, supplies of food-stuffs and agricultural raw materials will be available to industrial exporting nations only at increased cost in terms of manufactured goods. This means that densely populated areas may, in the more or less distant future, become poorer relatively to agricultural lands, and even absolutely. Considerations of this sort might induce a statesman to endorse protection for agriculture as a means of assuring a more favored future for an otherwise overcrowded country, but such matters are rather in the realm of clairvoyance than of reason.

The free trade thesis takes account only of total income and, to some extent, the sharing of it between nations.

It does not, and should not, consider the social arrangements under which that wealth is distributed among individuals. There is no tendency in free trade, as such, toward unequal distribution. On the contrary, this is at least as likely to happen under protection. In certain circumstances, however, protection, by encouraging industries which use a large amount of labor relative to land and equipment as compared with the industries which, under such protection, would suffer, may enlarge the *share* of the laboring class in the lowered national income and, *per contra* reduce the share of the *rentier*.[9] The laborer's larger share of the reduced total income might possibly be a greater absolute amount than he would otherwise receive. Class legislation of this sort may possibly be desirable on sociological grounds, though this, of course, is a quite open question. In any event it would seem to be better to secure the desired distribution by some means other than that which would involve a reduction in the total national income. Here also a *relaxation* of protection might, in other circumstances than those posited, accomplish the end for which protection is in the present case invoked.

Protection is at times used as a weapon to punish or prevent foreign discrimination, to force a more liberal trade policy on other nations, to serve as a retaliatory measure against restrictions which, though not discriminatory as between foreign nations, are regarded as un-

[9] All international trade tends, in any one of the countries concerned, to increase the relative value of such of the factors of production as are there comparatively plentiful (and therefore cheap) and to diminish the relative value of such of the factors as are there comparatively scarce (and therefore dear). The increase in total production and income will, however, almost surely lead to a higher absolute value, in terms of finished goods, of *all* of the productive factors.

due, and to establish a favorable bargaining position for prospective international commercial negotiations. The certain immediate loss to the levying country is not always recognized, but where it is, retaliatory duties are levied in the expectation that a still greater loss will be imposed on the foreign country against which they are specially aimed and that such country will thereby be persuaded to take a tractable attitude. In most cases this expectation is disappointed and the sole result is a competition in mutual injury. No doubt protection, as an instrument of economic strife, may sometimes have its uses, but it is a two-edged sword quite as likely to wound its wielder as the "enemy" against whom it is directed. In any event, when used for the purposes discussed in this paragraph, the object of the protective measures is not to restrict but to enlarge the freedom of commercial intercourse; it seeks to restrain restraints. The protection is then justified not on its own account but solely as a means of securing freer trade.

A similar defence may be made of protective or other duties levied in the prevention of dumping. To this subject more detailed attention will be given in the next chapter.

Diversification of industry as insurance is frequently put upon a military rather than an economic basis. An assured domestic supply of the materials of war, through the protection of manufacturing industries producing or capable of quick conversion to the production of munitions and other manufactured commodities in the panoply of Mars, is freely advocated in countries which, under a liberal commercial policy, would specialize in agriculture. On the other hand, countries whose comparative competence lies in manufacturing are often urged, for the sake of defence, to provide for the domestic production of necessary food-stuffs.

While diversification of output, provided it is not achieved at extremely high cost, may be desirable on military grounds, it may be worth while to point out that a country like Great Britain could never have shown the military power which it has, in fact, exerted, had it attempted to secure a domestic supply of food-stuffs and so reduced its *per capita* economic strength, or greatly limited its population, or both. Free trade here gave greater military power than protection could ever have done. Military power is, of course, not the same thing as invulnerability, and a strong navy has been felt to be essential to the keeping open of British avenues of trade which, under another policy, might never have existed or, at least, been of vital concern.

SUMMARY

If now we survey as a whole the various arguments for protection gathered in this chapter, we shall see that they are in some degree conflicting; that they are, for the most part, applicable only in special circumstances and for limited ends; and that, under different conditions, free trade might better promote even these ends than would the imposition of restraints. Except for the pleas against specialization, *qua* specialization, the arguments for protection could, in a differently constituted environment, be turned directly against that policy.[10] In

---

[10] The argument is not for protection as such but for the type of industry which, in given circumstances, protection would foster. It often appears in negative form as a protest against the composition of industry which, in given circumstances, tends to evolve under *laissez faire*. Change the circumstances, and the argument in both cases would support a free trade policy.

a complex situation a restrictive policy, rationally followed in the furtherance of any given purpose, will not only impose immediate losses but may very easily render more difficult of attainment some other cherished purpose. The protection of one industry, for instance, may injure another equally or more than equally desirable.

Whether the result of any given protective duty will or will not be favorable depends therefore not only upon a calculation of the inherent loss in the abandonment of productive specialization but upon the prospect of ulterior results, some of them not easily foreseeable, which are as likely as not to be economically unfavorable. The chances are therefore against a beneficial result, even for protection limited to specific and rigidly defined ends, while there is no prospect whatever of a favorable economic outcome of a widely extended protective policy. We can, indeed, never measure the results of protection since we can never know what would have happened had a different policy been pursued; but the deduction from any process of logic worthy of the name must be that protection can only hope to be useful by being confined to rather narrow, specific, and clearly defined purposes and that, even within these purposes, it has rather limited possibilities for good.

CHAPTER VI

ANTI-DUMPING LEGISLATION AND SPE-
CIAL FORMS OF FOREIGN TRADE CONTROL

THE NATURE OF DUMPING

DUMPING, scientifically defined as price discrimination between national markets,[1] is a phenomenon of monopoly of considerable but perhaps not increasing importance in international trade. Monopoly can be established either by private interests or by governmental activity. Since monopoly may make it profitable to discriminate in the prices charged to different buyers, a thing which would be practically impossible under conditions of perfectly free competition, the arguments for a *laissez-faire* trade policy, which are based on the assumption of such free competition, are, in the case of dumping, open to question.

The usual type of dumping, however, involves the sale of products to foreign consumers at discriminatingly *low* prices and, if the permanence of this situation could be assured, there would be no economic reason for restrictive legislation by countries subject to such dumping. This is true whether the import, at dumping prices, would or would not force a local industry to the wall. Whether the factors which lead to the prices of a coun-

[1] Cf. Jacob Viner, *Dumping: A Problem in International Trade*, University of Chicago Press, Chicago, 1923, p. 3.

try's imports being lower than domestic cost of production are natural or artificial is a matter of indifference to such country. Provided the situation will be permanent, it will in any case be economically advantageous to secure in foreign markets anything which can persistently be obtained more cheaply by the import-export process than by direct production within the home territory.[2]

Dumping, however, is so little likely to be permanent and is characteristically so predatory that there is a general disposition on the part of countries subjected to dumping to legislate against it. On the whole this disposition is to be approved. Except when conducted under the ægis of mercantilistic governments ready to assume losses indefinitely, dumping is likely to be sporadic, with the intention of getting rid of a casual surplus or of eliminating competition by financial might rather than by productivity. In neither of the latter cases is it likely to be in the long-run interest of the

---

[2] Where dumping is of the cost-reducing type, undertaken for the sake of securing lower unit costs by reason of the expansion of output for which such dumping offers a market, some interesting possibilities occur. It may not only be worth while for a given country to protect a comparatively incompetent industry subject to lower unit costs as output is enlarged (a matter treated in the preceding chapter) but it is theoretically possible that an industry comparatively incompetent at the point of production may, under a policy of price discrimination, be able to supply *all* consumers at lower prices than would be possible for a comparatively more competent industry differently situated. Whether, under the monopoly conditions which make price discrimination feasible, it will elect to do so is another question. The fact remains that the total *cost* of goods delivered to consumers may, in certain circumstances, be less if they are produced by plants which, under a *laissez-faire* trade policy, would never come into existence, than if they were produced by plants which, for a given volume of output, would show factory costs per unit consistently lower than their rivals. For an illustration of this point, see the special note at the end of this chapter.

recipient country. Dumped products, in general, may therefore be eliminated from the list of imports which, on economic principles, should be subject to no discrimination with respect to the source of supply. Anti-dumping legislation, properly drawn, is, in fact, a discrimination against discrimination, and this, except in rather unusual situations, is economically desirable.

"EXCHANGE DUMPING"

It is important, however, to be clear as to what constitutes dumping. Dumping is freely charged against any foreign producer who sells at a price which causes discomfort to domestic competitors. Whatever the price, however, there is no dumping in any precise use of the term so long as factory prices to all buyers are equal. This at once rules out so-called exchange dumping. Any country abandoning the gold standard is likely, in the early stages, to experience a comparatively heavy discount of its currency in the foreign exchange market. The recession from gold has been due, presumably, to a comparatively high price level with a tendency toward an increase in the ratio of commodity imports to commodity exports (aside from gold). The sudden and, as compared with internal purchasing power, excessive fall in the exchange value of the currency not only nullifies this tendency but usually exaggerates the change. The ensuing expansion of exports relative to imports then operates to reverse the downward movement in the exchange value of the currency in question and to bring it up to the point at which equilibrium between its external and internal value is attained. The mechanism is self-equilibrating.

There is at no time anything in the process which can properly be described as dumping. All purchasers pay the same price, but foreigners happen to be able temporarily to buy the requisite currency cheaply. To expose to special restrictive legislation the exports of a country whose currency, in terms of foreign exchange, is temporarily cheap is to perpetuate the evil such legislation seeks to combat. The only effective way to raise the exchange value of a currency unduly depressed is to have an increase in the ratio of exports to imports of the country to which that currency appertains. If its exports are restricted by special legislation in other countries, the exchange value of the currency is likely to show a persistently falling tendency relative to internal purchasing power and thus to make the so-called dumping continuous. If the ratio of exports to imports of any one country is too low for equilibrium, the same ratio in some other country or countries must be too high. To block the adjustment which automatically tends to occur through a movement in exchange rates is, therefore, to cherish instability and invite collapse.[8]

The erring but general tendency to regard exports as desirable and imports as at best a necessary evil is responsible for the disposition, so manifest in recent years, toward a persistent competition in exchange depreciation. It is possible, by progressive inflation, to keep the

---

[8] Attempts not to prevent but to retard the adjustment may, however, be justified. This is one of the cases where a sudden change may produce violent dislocations. Emergency measures on the part of countries subjected to a great increase of certain imports, at low prices, from countries with an unduly depressed foreign exchange value on their currencies, may be desirable if they are not prohibitory but are designed merely to serve as checks on a temporary or runaway process which threatens the currency of the recipient country. The time factor here, as elsewhere, must be taken into consideration.

exchange value of a currency below its value in the domestic market (its value at home higher than on the exchanges) as long as the home population distrusts the currency less than foreigners do. So far, however, as the exchange value of a currency is kept below its internal purchasing power, the country in question is selling its exports at a sacrifice in terms of imports.

The issue of this process is ruin, as the record clearly shows in the case of Germany from the end of the World War till late in 1923. Germany was at that time an immense bargain counter for foreign buyers and was so drained of goods that the German government was impelled to put an end to the German "advantage" in foreign trade, to *force* German exporters to raise their prices, and to discriminate against exports by a differential which favored the home consumer.

It is also possible to keep the exchange value of a free currency low relative to gold standard currencies if the country in question is willing to absorb unlimited quantities of gold. The competition in exchange depreciation in more recent years is one aspect of that passion for gold which has been so destructive of the true ends of economic activity. Countries which have abandoned the gold standard are often still so eager to acquire gold that the holders of the currency of such countries are ready to sell it against gold for much less than its real worth. The great source of gold is in the reserves of the countries which still remain on the gold standard. The depreciation of free in terms of gold currencies, as compared with their purchasing power over goods in their respective centers of circulation, means that the ratio of the ordinary commodity exports to the imports of gold standard countries tends to fall, the balance being paid in the gold which the other countries so urgently seek.

Carried to its conclusion, this will put all countries off the gold standard.[4] Gold from bank reserves being then no longer attainable, the principal stimulus and prerequisite to exchange depreciation would cease to exist and, except through a completely futile accumulation of unredeemed claims on foreign currencies, it would be impossible to keep one currency so low in terms of another as to lead to any special advantage in export markets. Every increase in the ratio of exports to imports which accrued to any country as a result of a relatively low exchange value for its currency would automatically elevate that rate. The competition in exchange depreciation, the so-called exchange dumping and the acquisition of temporary competitive advantages, is therefore not only attended by national losses even to the "successful" participants[5] but it is sooner or later practically impossible of continuance.

---

[4] Many protective duties have been imposed in recent years as emergency measures for the preservation of the currency. For reasons elsewhere given they are of little value for this purpose; but the pressure on the part of the affected industries, combined with the general fear of currency disturbance, has overridden all coldly conceived counsels.

[5] It is true that the excessive stimulus to exports which it affords may provide employment in certain industries which would otherwise be idle; and this, in itself, is a gain to the country concerned. But, in a state of world-wide unemployment, such activity is likely to be at the immediate expense of similar export industries in other countries, and their loss will be attended by a lack of purchasing power over external products which is almost certain to react on the foreign demand, in general, for the export commodities of the country whose export trade was originally favored. The only real solution of the difficulty is a general stimulus to activity which will operate equally in the domestic, export, and import fields for all the countries concerned.

Another type of alleged dumping is frequently charged against the Soviet government. The Soviet government, with its monopoly of foreign trade, is in a position to practice dumping on a large scale if it should wish to do so. But the Russian economic structure being what it is, it is hard to see how the Russians could obtain any economic benefit by dumping, and there seems to be no real evidence that they have ever practiced it on any great scale.[6]

To determine whether or not there is dumping from Russia is, however, extraordinarily difficult since the lack of free domestic markets, and a freely established exchange rate between Russian and other currencies, make an accurate comparison of internal and external prices out of the question. The best test of Russian dumping would be indirect, through a comparison of the ratio between the rouble price of any two Russian commodities in the principal domestic market with that of the foreign exchange price at which they were offered to consumers in the outside world. If these ratios deviate from equality there is *prima facie* evidence of dumping.

The Russians, however, have a very realistic attitude toward exports in that they regard them solely as a means for the acquisition of imported supplies. They are therefore prone to develop foreign commerce along much the same lines as would evolve under a non-

---

[6] At times, nevertheless, when the Russians have been in urgent need of foreign exchange to pay for imports on which contracts had already been signed, they may have indulged in practices which, without an undue stretching of the concept, could be held to constitute dumping.

monopolistic capitalist regime, with protection for those industries which the Russians are building up, not indirectly by means of tariffs, but by direct control of foreign trade. To secure desired imports in the largest measure it is obviously better to send out those products which can be produced most cheaply in Russia, relative to the price which they will command abroad, and so long as this policy is pursued there will be no Russian dumping. The Russians are unlikely to sell goods abroad more cheaply than is necessary; and, with foreign trade under a single control which is also responsible for the provision of goods to domestic consumers, there could be no possible economic motive for selling, at a given price to foreign buyers, that one of two or more commodities which is the more highly valued at home.[7] Russia may well sell certain commodities at lower prices than competing countries think desirable. There is nothing peculiar about this, however, and it is as favorable to buyers as it is detested by competing sellers.

The control of foreign trade, in Russia or elsewhere, has its menacing aspect, but dumping is not one of the potential dangers except in an incidental way. It would, for instance, be possible for the Russians to manipulate speculative produce markets by heavy short sales followed by dumping of the product on a scale sufficient to break the cash, and consequently the speculative, market. Such dumping need not approach in volume the amount of short sales and it would permit the latter to be covered at a substantial profit. Several years ago the Russians were charged with this practice in the Chicago wheat market, but the charges were never adequately proven and succeeding events have rather gone to show

[7] The prospect of Russian dumping, if any, must be associated with political rather than economic motives.

that the Soviet grain administration merely sold while the market was comparatively good, leaving other holders of wheat to wait in vain, for years, for a rise in prices.

National control of foreign trade, by permitting the shifting of supplies or orders *in toto* from one market to another, also furnishes a potent bargaining weapon which is subject to great abuse. The Soviet practice in this matter has been followed by many other nations in recent years in the system of exchange control, of quotas or contingents of imports from given countries or of given products, and of similar devices, all of which run counter to the spirit of equality of treatment of one foreign nation with another and seemingly to the letter of treaties guaranteeing such equality.

All of these controls, moreover, deviate from the principle that in every country there is an appropriate ratio between the volume of foreign and domestic trade,[8] and that this ratio is most likely to be closely approximated if no restraints are put upon foreign commerce other than those which, for one reason or another, are laid upon domestic transactions. Just as foreign trade

---

[8] The ratio appropriate to any given country may be great or small according to differing circumstance. Any country which can produce within its own borders, at cost ratios approximately equal to those which prevail in the world at large, the bulk of the products which it consumes, will tend to show a low appropriate ratio of foreign to domestic trade. Many factors contribute to this situation, among which may be mentioned the size of the country, the variety of its resources, its shape, orientation, nearness to foreign markets, transport facilities, and the like. A country of approximately circular shape, for instance, will tend to show a small appropriate ratio of foreign to domestic trade as compared with a country whose shape is more nearly linear; while a linear-shaped country stretching north and south, and thus securing a varied climate, will tend to show a similarly small appropriate ratio as compared with a country of like shape with an east and west orientation.

should not, in general, be restrained by discriminations, neither should it be so encouraged as, for instance, by bounties, dumping, and similar practices. Such discriminations are usually haphazard, without rational basis in the common interest, and evil in their consequences to the discriminating as to other nations.

BILATERAL EQUIVALENCE OF EXPORTS AND IMPORTS

One of the most vicious types of discrimination is that which is devoted to securing equality of exports and imports as between one country and *each* of the other countries of the world. The notion that imports from any foreign country should be confined to an amount equal to the domestic exports to that country is childish. It is analogous to the situation in which a chewing-gum magnate, on the purchase of an expensive automobile, should insist that the automobile manufacturer reciprocate by buying from him for his own use an equivalent value of chewing gum.

The *total* foreign income and outlay of every solvent nation must balance; but to expect that there should be a balance in all the parts is ridiculous. No country buys from another, in larger measure than it sells, for any other reason than that it is in its own interest to do so. To insist upon bilateral equivalence in the exports and imports of any given country with *each* of the others is to force international trade into extremely costly channels or to render it altogether impossible. Most of the advantages of specialization along lines of comparative competence are then lost since there is not one chance in millions that the appropriate specialization of production in the several countries will coincide with an equivalence of imports and exports between each of them.

British Malaya sends rubber to the United States to a large value every year, but it would be foolish for the United States to insist that that country import an equivalent value of American products. The inhabitants of Malaysia have no strong predilection for the type of production in which the United States specializes and, even if they had, a sizable part of the proceeds of their rubber exports accrues to British and other non-Malaysian owners of plantations so that purchasing power over foreign commodities does not accrue to the Malaysians in anything like the full measure of their exports. The dollar proceeds of the sales of rubber to the United States are sold by their recipients to the highest bidders, whatever their nationality, and must be used to purchase American commodities. The purchasers of this dollar exchange (the purchase being typically made with goods sold to Malaysia) thus buy more American goods than they could get if their acquisition of dollars were limited to the supplies available from exports of their own country to the United States. It is a matter of indifference to the latter country whether the actual buyers of so much of its export as is sent out in payment for purchases of rubber are or are not natives of Malaysia. To insist that they should be would simply be to increase the cost of rubber to American consumers, and of American exports to British Malaya, without any compensating benefit to either country.

RECIPROCITY VS. MOST-FAVORED-NATION TREATMENT

A form of foreign trade control of increasing popularity is that associated with reciprocity agreements of one type or another. Such agreements require the modification or abrogation of any unconditional most-favored-nation treaties which may stand in the way. Most-favored-nation treaties are intended to prevent discrimination by guaranteeing to *all* the contracting parties as favorable treatment as is granted to any. When the network of treaties containing the most-favored-nation clause is widely extended the result is to eliminate special favors altogether. Most-favored-nation treaties, as such, are of no effect in securing low, or no, protective duties; they merely provide that, whatever the height of such duties, they shall be equal as between all the countries engaged.

It is alleged in responsible quarters that these treaties prevent a liberalizing of tariff schedules, inasmuch as there are said to be numerous pairs of countries which would be ready to grant each other reciprocal concessions in tariff rates but which are unwilling to generalize these concessions to the extent which existing most-favored-nation treaties require.

Any reduction in the protective schedules now strangling world commerce seems, *prima facie,* highly desirable; but to secure it through discrimination might well prove even more disastrous than no action at all. Reciprocity, in form, may be benevolent or malign; but even when, as between the parties concerned, it is an exchange of favors rather than of injuries it must discriminate *against* all those outside its scope. Protests are inevitable and, if unheeded, are likely to be followed by retaliation developing into that most vicious form of reciprocity—tariff wars.

Even if such wars can be prevented it does not follow that reductions of duty as between given countries, to the exclusion of others, will either promote foreign trade as a whole or lead to a better utilization of productive resources. It may, in fact, have just the opposite effect. Both the contracting parties to a reciprocity treaty may, as a result of the treaty, divert their productive resources into lines of comparative incompetence solely because each is sheltered in the markets of the other. The diversion may easily be greater with relatively low but discriminatory tariff schedules than with a higher range of duties equally applicable to imports from no matter what foreign source.[9]

The vogue of reciprocity proceeds largely from the fallacy of supposing that any one nation grants a favor to another when it imports goods therefrom and that it should therefore be accorded a similar favor in return. Since, however, imports are not made except in the interest of the importer and of his country, the buyer no more confers a favor than does the seller. Unilateral reductions of general protective tariffs are quite as advantageous to the reducing as to other countries, and there are seldom any good reasons why such reductions should not be made available to all comers.

Reciprocity may, in the present state of world opinion, be a useful weapon for securing, by stages, general tariff reductions.[10] There is, however, no real need for it since the virtue of reductions of protective schedules by any one country is in no way dependent on counter reductions by other countries; and such counter reductions, which would give additional advantages to all concerned, can be induced quite as well by a failure to negotiate or renew most-favored-nation treaties as by

---

[9] For an excellent discussion of this topic, cf. Jacob Viner, *The Most-favored-nation Clause, Index*, Vol. VI, No. 61, Stockholm, 1931. Professor Viner conclusively demonstrates that all of the alleged advantages of reciprocity may be obtained without discrimination involving the abrogation of most-favored-nation treaties.

[10] In support of this view, cf. F. W. Taussig, *Foreign Affairs*, Vol. II, No. 3, 1933.

discarding the latter altogether in favor of a system of discrimination between different sources of *foreign* supply.

All of the more recent devices in the control of foreign trade are aspects of the resurgence of protection since the World War of 1914-1918, which is itself but the culmination of a trend toward economic nationalism under way for more than half a century. Some of the causes of this neo-mercantilism are obvious. War always releases nationalistic passions; and in the state of high tension which characterized the period after 1920, the military arguments for protection have assumed enhanced importance. The breaking of certain large states into fragments, and the consequent growth of two or more protective structures where only one grew before, have also contributed greatly to economic separatism.

This, however, is by no means the whole story. The more deeply underlying motive is a groping toward security not only against the dangers of political warfare but against the vicissitudes of a world economic order, far from stable, and beyond the reach of any single state.

The groping has, for the most part, been misguided, since attempts at economic autarchy in any one country have but increased the difficulties of others with later adverse repercussions on the initiating state. The solidarity of the economic world as it is now organized inevitably visits disaster upon those who essay to disrupt it. It is impossible, however, to look without sympathy on the many efforts now being made to provide a less shaky foundation for economic welfare. Since the world does not yet seem ready for concerted action in the solution of its major economic problems, attention is inevitably directed toward action on a national basis.

If there were any convincing evidence that the fluctuations in a nationalistic economy could be made less violent than those which must be presumed to be likely to continue to afflict the world at large, the insurance argument for self-sufficiency would here have cogency. Though self-sufficiency would mean a reduction of the national income below the *potential* level under a liberal commercial policy, it would not necessarily, over a period of years, diminish actually realized national returns. Greater steadiness, moreover, would be a distinct gain even at the expense of some reduction in the total. Except in the case of a small number of specially situated, not necessarily large, countries, there is small reason for believing, however, that the attainment of thoroughgoing self-sufficiency is other than an idle dream. There is still less reason for supposing that it would give the stability at which it aims. If, on the other hand, stability *within* any large country can be achieved by other means, it is not likely to be seriously menaced by a liberal trade policy. The disposition to withdraw from international trade is merely a phase of the tendency, when things go wrong, to blame the foreigner. There is no real ground for believing that the presence of international trade has materially increased the post-war difficulties of any country. On the contrary, the restrictions placed upon it have played a very vicious rôle.

Aside from honestly intended emergency measures to prevent a shifting of trade currents and of industrial structures in response to *temporary* storms arising from disturbed currency conditions or the like, the post-war systems of control are nothing but a tragic nuisance.

All control of foreign trade implies a conscious or unconscious aim of some sort, but it will usually be found that the aim is perverse or that the practices by which realization thereof is sought are abortive. Clear-eyed pursuit of a rational policy is rare, and there is, in general, no disposition to look through catchwords into the realities of welfare. "Control" is appealing regardless of its purpose or results and, in the field of foreign trade, is quite generally based on wholly untenable premises. This is the more generally true when it involves special favors to some, and therefore disfavors to other, foreign nations.

NOTE ON SOME PHASES OF DUMPING

Let us suppose two countries, Ex and Fourex, each with an inelastic demand for a given product, the developed demand of Fourex being four times that of Ex. The industry meeting this demand is first established in Ex and, *with a given volume of output*, would always be able to produce at lower cost per unit than any similar industry in Fourex could do. Since the market of Ex is only ¼ as large as that of Fourex, however, it is quite possible that a producer in Fourex, provided he has a monopoly of the market in his own country, may be able to produce at lower unit costs than a producer in Ex who is excluded from Fourex and can sell only in his own limited home territory. Moreover, dumping is a much more feasible policy for the producer in Fourex than for the producer in Ex since the former would cut prices only on 1/5 of his output and make up for this cut on the 4/5 of the total production consumed domestically, while *the latter would be subjected to the reverse conditions.* If we assume a scale of costs as in the subjoined table, and suppose that

Conditions	Unit Cost in Ex	Unit Cost in Fourex
Initiation......................	$1.14	$1.40
With only a fully developed domestic market available to a single producer..................	1.08	1.02
With fully developed markets in both countries available to a single producer	.85	.94

the cost of transport per unit in either direction is \$.16, then it is clear that if the industry were first developed in Ex, and access to the market of Fourex were free, no producer in Fourex could ever become established. Minimum prices, with the producer in Ex supplying both markets, would be \$.85 per unit in Ex and \$1.01 (.85 + .16) per unit in Fourex. If a prohibitive duty on imports were imposed by Fourex, the cost per unit of production in that country would not fall to the delivered price (\$1.01) at which it could otherwise be obtained from Ex unless the producer in Fourex could secure the market in Ex, in which case it would fall considerably below (to \$.94). He could secure this market by dumping. All he need do is beat the price, \$1.08, which is the cost per unit in Ex when production is confined to the home market. A price at the Fourex factory of \$.92— per unit to consumers in Ex will be sufficient. Since costs, under these conditions, will be \$.94 per unit, the loss of \$.02+ per unit on the 1/5 of total production sold in Ex must be compensated by ½c per unit additional price on the 4/5 of total production sold in Fourex. Any price between \$.945 and \$1.02 in Fourex, with dumping at a delivered price just below \$1.08 in Ex, will yield larger profits to the producer in Fourex, and will give to consumers in both countries a cheaper supply, than could be obtained by production, for sale in home markets only, at \$1.08 and \$1.02 respectively.

It would even be possible for the producer in Fourex to sell in both markets at a lower price than would be possible, on a non-dumping basis, with production for both markets carried on in Ex. If the producer in Fourex sells at factory for \$.69— per unit to consumers in Ex, the product can be landed in the latter country at something less than \$.85 per unit. To sell at \$.69— per unit at factory in Fourex involves a loss of \$.25+ per unit on the dumped supply. This would be compensated by an increase of \$.0625+ per unit in the supply sold at home. Add this to cost (\$.94 per unit), and the price in Fourex could still be below the \$1.01 delivered cost in Fourex of supplies from Ex when the latter country is producing for both markets.

We thus have the somewhat surprising result of production in the country of high cost, stimulated by protection and accompanied by dumping, making it possible for all consumers to get their supplies more cheaply than could otherwise occur. This is true because producers in Ex have not the same potentialities in dumping as have those in Fourex. For every cent below the $1.01 delivered price at which the producer in Ex sells in Fourex he must raise the price to his domestic consumers above his $.85 unit cost by $.04. To sell for $1.00 delivered price per unit in Fourex he must therefore get at least $.89 at home. But if the producer in Fourex were to sell for $.89 per delivered unit in Ex he could afford to take something *less* than $1.00 per unit in Fourex. (The net price at factory to consumers in Ex would be $.73 per unit, a loss of $.21 per unit. This would be compensated by an increase of $.0525 per unit over the $.94 unit cost on supplies sold in Fourex.) Similarly, with any other set of discriminatory prices, consumers could be supplied at lower unit delivered cost from Fourex than from Ex.

It should be further noted that if the price in Ex, for a volume of production sufficient to supply the home market only, should happen to be $1.10+ per unit instead of $1.08, the producer in Fourex could eventually provide for both markets, *without dumping*, at lower *total* cost than under any alternative method of supply. The price in Fourex would be $.94 per unit and, in Ex, $1.10. This would be lower than with production in both countries for their own markets. But even with production in Ex for both markets, the $.25 per unit reduction to consumers in Ex (unit price $.85 instead of $1.10) would be more than balanced by the $.07 per unit increase to the fourfold as many consumers in Fourex (unit price $1.01 instead of $.94). Protection of a comparatively incompetent industry of declining unit costs as output is expanded may therefore, in certain circumstances, not only be advantageous to consumers in the levying country but may eventually permit such an industry, though still comparatively incompetent in the technical sense, to supply all consumers, taken as a whole, more cheaply than would otherwise be possible, and, when combined with dumping, may make it possible to sell at lower prices to every individual consumer than under any alternative distribution of production.

CHAPTER VII

THE FUTURE COMMERCIAL POLICY OF THE UNITED STATES

THE prospects of general benefit from a protectionist policy are, as preceding chapters have shown, much stronger in some environments than in others. The immediate loss issuing from such a policy may sometimes be expected to be more than compensated by accruing economic advantages in the transfer from a rural to an urban economy, from specialization in agriculture to a more widely diversified productive structure, and in other situations more or less fully exemplified in the history of the American Union up to the beginning of the twentieth century.

There is, however, little if any excuse for protection in the United States at the present day. Hardly any of the special pleas for protection developed in Chapter V apply to the existing situation. In so highly industrialized a country, with capital as cheap as in any part of the world, with a great volume of manufactured exports, and with new manufacturing industries developing in free competition with other nations, the argument for nurturing protection becomes all but ridiculous. No one will maintain that our manufacturing industries are still puny children in need of nurture until they can acquire strength, or that our finance is infantile, in other than a derisive sense. There is now no probability whatever that, under any conceivable commercial policy, industry in the United States would fail to be so diversified as to give scope to whatever talents American citizens may possess. All industries important for defence are already fully developed within the continental area or are incapable of ever finding lodgment there. There is not the slightest reason for supposing that the terms of trade on which the United States carries on its commerce with foreign nations are so improved by protection as to compensate the loss from diversion of effort to relatively disadvantageous industries. Similarly, the protection associated with the development of pursuits presenting a negatively inclined social or entrepreneurial cost curve (decreasing cost per unit) has probably exhausted the possibilities available, while changing comparative competence has made it unlikely that a reversal of the policy of prohibitory duties would, in the long run, be attended by any losses. We may at present, indeed, be well within the stage of rising cost per unit of output as concentration of population proceeds.

Natural resources, moreover, are now somewhat more likely to be conserved through a liberal than through a restrictive commercial policy.[1] If agriculture is a peculiarly desirable industry for a country to have, its prosperity in the United States would be much more assured under a generally liberal trade policy than through an attempt to cover certain branches of agriculture by

[1] This is evidenced by the agitation for protective duties on certain important mineral raw materials of which we have hitherto been exporters. Their continued free import would tend to prevent as rapid a use of the home supplies of these wasting assets as would take place under protection.

protection. As long as our great agricultural staples are on an export basis, the level of farmer income, even in the branches of agricultural production in which the country fails to provide fully for its own consumption, cannot over any extended period rise above that obtained by producers of agricultural exports. For as soon as it does, a movement out of export crops and into the protected lines is initiated, and continued until no more is to be earned in one crop than in another.[2]

Protection, in general, unless accompanied by monopoly, does not raise the incomes even of the protected producers above those of producers in non-protected lines, and it always tends to lower incomes as a whole. Protection simply makes it possible for producers in relatively incompetent branches of industry to secure the going rate of return. It does so by lowering the real return in the relatively more competent branches of industry more than it raises the real return in the less competent. The strongest ground of complaint by exporting industries against the levy or increase of effective protection for other industries is not that the cost of living is increased thereby without a corresponding increase of income. This is true for *everyone*, including those who shift to some one of the newly protected industries; and, on this score, exporting industries have no *special* grievance.[3] But effective protection, by shutting out foreign goods and thus automatically cutting

[2] Land values, however, may be affected; and the landowner, whether he be a farmer or not, might benefit, at the expense of the population at large, from a policy of agricultural protection.

[3] The rise in the cost of living tends, however, to result in a somewhat less than proportionate rise in *money* wages in the export industries, and this increase in the entrepreneur's costs cannot readily be compensated by an enhancement of the prices at which exported products are sold.

off a foreign market for exports, forces existing exporters either to take a cut in prices which will result in selling abroad the same volume of goods for a greatly reduced money return or to abandon part of the export market altogether.

In times when population is rapidly increasing and when all existing lines of production are therefore being expanded, the restriction upon exports involved in protection tends to express itself only in a retardation of the rate of growth rather than in any absolute decline. But when, as at present, population has ceased to show a rapid rate of augmentation, absolute declines in certain existing export industries, among which agriculture is prominent, can seemingly be avoided only by the transition to a more liberal tariff policy.

RELATIONS BETWEEN INTERNATIONAL TRADE AND INTERNATIONAL FINANCE

The pressure, in restriction of exports, of a policy of protective import duties increases as a country moves into a net creditor position on international financial account. International commercial policy bears a definite relationship to international finance. Whenever, in any country, net interest payments to foreign countries are in excess of net current borrowing from abroad, or whenever net new lending to foreign countries surpasses in volume net receipts of interest from external sources, and the country in question is thus subject, on capital account, to an excess of claims on its currency over its own claims on foreign currencies, the condition of solvency is a corresponding net credit in the other international economic transactions of the given country. An excess of current exports of goods and services over similar imports is called for. Restraints on imports are then in line with the trend of economic forces, and a protectionist policy at such a time is much less likely to provoke disturbance than in the contrary situation.

However, when a country, either because its net borrowing abroad is in excess of its current net interest payments to foreign countries or because its net receipts of interest from abroad are in excess of its new external lending, has a net current excess of claims on capital account, the condition of international solvency is a corresponding net deficit of claims in its other international economic transactions. An excess of current imports of goods and services over similar exports is called for. To then impose widespread restraints on imports and thus attempt to lower the ratio of exports to imports, is to fight the trend of economic forces and is likely to lead to financial and economic disaster.

ADJUSTMENT OF POLICY TO CHANGING CONDITIONS

The history of the United States clearly illustrates these propositions. The settlement of the West, with the building of roads, railroads, and canals in the decades between 1820 and the Civil War, set up a demand for capital which resulted in heavy borrowing abroad and therefore in a tendency toward an excess of commodity imports over commodity exports. In these circumstances the highly protective tariff system inaugurated in 1816 began to play a very vicious rôle, and the consequent drive for lower duties resulted in a progressive liberalization of our tariff schedules until the outbreak of hostilities in 1861. Such a liberal tariff policy facilitated the high ratio of imports to exports which characterized this period.

Foreign borrowing was sharply curtailed after the panic of 1873[4] and, since interest payments on old loans were still required, the necessity for an excess of merchandise imports was changed into the necessity for a surplus of merchandise exports.[5] The policy of thoroughgoing restrictions on imports pursued in this country since Civil War days was not, therefore, entirely inappropriate to the general situation existing from 1873 till after the World War.

This does not mean that either a free trade or a protectionist policy is inevitable in certain situations and impossible in others. Either may be followed under almost any external conditions. The ratio of commodity imports to exports will, through movements in relative national price levels, automatically adjust itself to whatever commercial policy may be adopted. Under a free trading regime the import-export ratio will be flexible, while under protection it will be much more rigid. However, where capital movements require a surplus of commodity imports in any given country, and such a country lays drastic restrictions on the entry of foreign goods, adjustment will ordinarily occur through a decline in sales of exports sufficient to keep the ratio of imports to exports high even though imports are greatly curtailed by the restrictive policy imposed. If, nevertheless, imports are excluded *wholly*, or to such a degree as to amount in value to less than the net income due on

---

[4] This panic may well have been, in large measure, induced by the contradiction between a net borrowing position on current capital items and the shift in commercial policy, introduced during the Civil War, toward restrictive measures against imports.

[5] Other factors, such as the decline in the American mercantile marine and the growth of "tourism" among Americans, later worked toward the same result.

capital account, an international financial collapse is inevitable. For, even if exports should then sink to zero, there could be no excess of imports adequate to effect the payments on capital account due to the country in question.

Under a liberal commercial policy there is no analogous difficulty when the items in capital account call for an equilibrating excess of commodity and service *exports*. Relative national price levels will then readily adjust themselves so as to provoke a more than even ratio of exports to imports whatever the volume of the imports may be. As far as reconciliation of the phenomena of international trade with those of international finance is concerned, therefore, a liberal commercial policy is *always* fitting, while a protectionist policy is merely less inappropriate to a situation in which an excess of exports on merchandise account is required to balance an excess of imports on capital account than it is to the converse status.

The large loans made to foreign countries during and after the World War accentuated the tendency toward an excess of commodity exports over imports, and the protective policy against imports therefore remained for a time comparatively innocuous. Rising interest payments, however, and a decline in the disposition of Americans to continue foreign lending on the scale of the early post-war years, have completely altered the situation.

The United States is now in the later phases of a cycle of international capital movements in which it appeared first as a net borrower, then as a net payer of interest in excess of new borrowings (later attended by repayments of former borrowings), then as a net lender, and finally as a net recipient of interest.[6] The net excess of foreign claims to United States currency over American claims in the opposite direction which marked the international *financial* account from 1873 almost to the present is the basis for the notion of the "traditional" character of an excess of *commodity* exports over imports, and of a highly protective tariff policy, in the United States. The turning point was apparently reached in 1929. It is true that, if the people of the United States resume foreign lending on a scale sufficient, along with interest payments and amortization on American securities held by foreigners, to outweigh such receipts of interest, dividends, and amortization payments as accrue to them on obligations of foreigners, the excess of American exports on merchandise account will tend for some time to continue. This, however, does not seem likely and is, in any case, incapable of indefinite extension. If the much more probable decline in American foreign lending (and other overseas transmission of capital items from this country), relative to interest and other inflowing capital items, now takes place, an excess of imports on merchandise account seems bound

---

[6] In the years prior to 1929 the trend, apart from the very large foreign investments by residents of the United States, was toward an increasing ratio of imports to exports. It would have been well if the structure of American and foreign industry had been gradually adapted to this situation. Instead of developing an economic structure in the United States consonant with a net import status, and an economic structure abroad consonant with a net export status in the debtor countries, American foreign lending, on a suddenly expanded scale, was of such a volume as to promote a trend in national economic structures quite contrary to that requisite to long-run equilibrium. The result was disaster as soon as the volume of American loans declined. The various national industrial structures having been developed in exactly the opposite direction to that appropriate to the evolving situation, the difficulties of adjustment were made extreme.

to occur at an early date and, in any event, can apparently be postponed to no very distant future.

There is no reason why it should be postponed. The artificial restriction of imports runs counter to a fundamental financial trend in the opposite direction,[7] increases rather than reduces friction, and not only prevents the growth of exports but may impose upon them an absolute decline. Where supply is inelastic, as in agricultural output, this decline is at first likely to take the form of so sharp a drop in values that the same, or even an increased, volume of exports will be worth less than before. Provided highly protective tariffs are maintained, it is only, therefore, after a long period of low prices and distress that exports will be sufficiently diminished (through the elimination of some of the suppliers by bankruptcy) to permit export prices again to rise to the level appropriate to the new equilibrium.

Highly protective tariffs in the United States will now, in all probability, thus effect a collapse in exports disproportionate to the limitation of imports, or will make international financial payments impossible, or both.[8] A certain amount of imports will be required to furnish solvent foreigners with the means of payment of their more or less fixed obligations on financial account with the United States. The more we restrict imports the nearer we shall get to the point where all

---

[7] In so far as interest and dividends are being, or will be, paid on American foreign investments to an amount greater than the annual volume of new foreign lending by citizens of this country.

[8] The one great possibility of adjustment, with the maintenance of high protection, is a wholly unprecedented expansion of "tourism" on the part of Americans. The growth of American travel abroad since the World War has, however, gone a long way toward effecting adjustment between the conflicting policies of expansion of commodity exports and restriction of commodity imports of the ordinary type.

of the proceeds of the imports which we still permit will be necessary for this purpose. We should then be traveling the road toward complete elimination of exports, and the international price situation would so adjust itself as automatically to bring this state of affairs ever closer to realization. So great an absolute reduction in exports, however, could be accomplished only at enormous cost in rendering existing fixed capital worthless, in unemployment, and in all similar frictional losses.

An indispensable prerequisite to a liberal tariff policy is a revolution in the popular attitude toward imports. Instead of looking upon imports as a more or less necessary evil we must be prepared to welcome them as the sole rational end of foreign trade. Exports are the means of providing for imports and, from the national point of view, they have no other function. A tariff policy, grotesquely named "scientific," which, through the levy of a protective duty on potential imports, seeks a general equalization of costs of production (that is, of costs of delivery in the United States), is absurd. It is only because costs, and prices, on some products are lower abroad than in the United States (with its corollary of costs and prices of other products being lower in the United States than abroad) that there is any advantage in carrying on foreign trade. No more perverted notion than that the way to prosperity is to make it necessary to spend more than the minimum to secure a given product has ever afflicted a great nation.

MEASUREMENT OF THE TARIFF BURDEN

To estimate with precision the burden of protection in the United States upon the consumer (to say nothing of that on the producer of exports) is, for reasons which cannot here be taken up, a matter of great difficulty. Some of the attempts at such an estimate, by high officials of administrations of the not distant past, were hopelessly naïve or deliberately disingenuous. It was alleged, for instance, that the "average" rate of duty might be found by taking the percentage relationship between total duties collected and the total value of existing imports. The absurdity of this procedure will be obvious when we reflect that certain goods come in free of duty, and that if, on all other goods, protective duties were raised to absolutely prohibitive levels, there would be no duties collected at all. On the basis of the official reasoning we should then reach the conclusion that, in the presence of a wide range of duties so high as altogether to exclude the articles affected, the "average" rate of duty was zero.

A "refinement" of this procedure takes the total of duties collected as a percentage of the total value of dutiable products actually imported and declares this to be the "average" rate of duty. This is, in truth, an average of a sort but it is very far from expressing the general height of tariff schedules. On most dutiable products our tariff schedules have for long years been practically prohibitive. On some they were not. The lower the duty, relative to the price of the product in bond, the more likely are imports to occur. The tendency, therefore, is for the only duties collected to be those which form a very moderate percentage of the value of the product concerned. The ratio of total collections to total value of goods imported would therefore be low when a policy of almost complete exclusion of imports, through a generally towering range of protective duties, is followed. Such a ratio could easily fall as a result of an *increase* in duties which prevented the import of commodities which had formerly been able to surmount a somewhat lower barrier.

It might seem possible to compute the real height of a tariff schedule by taking an average of the actually existing rates. It makes no real difference, however, whether a rate is 100 per cent or 1000 per cent if both are prohibitive. A rate of 5 per cent, moreover, might exclude some products, whereas 500 per cent would not exclude others. The real question is not the absolute height of the rate but whether or not it excludes the import of the whole or a part of the domestic consumption of the commodity affected.

It has, in the past, been officially urged that our protective wall is not really high because a very large proportion of our imports comes in free.[9] The question can again be raised whether, with a limited free list, with all other products subject to prohibitively high rates, and all of such imports as occur therefore entering free of duty, we should conclude that we had no tariff barriers. It must be clear that the reason why about two-thirds of our existing imports have been those on the free list is that these are the only goods which we have been disposed to let in at all.[10]

A high proportion of free to dutiable imports could never show that a tariff policy was liberal but rather that it was practically exclusive of all those things on which duties were imposed. The burden of a protective duty must not be determined on the basis of the goods which

---

[9] These are almost entirely raw materials of industry or food products not produced in the United States. Their free entry is perfectly consistent with—nay, even an expression of—a thoroughgoing protectionist policy.

[10] Of the dutiable imports, sugar yields a major part of the revenues collected; and, at present prices of sugar (1933), the duty runs between 200 and 300 per cent.

come in but on that of those which are shut out. To the extent that goods come in over a duty there is no protection, nor, so far as this part of the supply is concerned, is there any national burden. The consumer pays more but the government gets the difference and can presumably relax the pressure of other taxes correspondingly.

But, under effective protection, the consumer pays more, the government gets nothing, and the producer makes no more than he could make in such export industries as would develop under free trading conditions. The extra price paid by the consumer is eaten up in high costs. The real burden is the difference between the total real income which could be respectively obtained under a comparatively self-sufficing and a specialized system. The real height of a protective tariff wall can be gauged, even approximately, only by the difference in the price of any given commodity as it is in the protected market and as it would be in that market if the duty were removed.

THE POSSIBILITY OF UNILATERAL LIBERALISM IN TARIFF POLICY

There is no ground for believing that the adoption of a really liberal tariff policy in this country would do other than improve our standard of living. Neither in theory nor in fact is there any support for the notion that we could now or in the future improve, or even maintain, that standard by means of tariffs. This is true whether or not other countries adopt, maintain, or renounce a protectionist policy. Holland, one of the most prosperous countries in Europe, has persistently maintained a substantially free trade position in the face of rising tariff barriers in the outside world and is certainly none the worse for it. Its prosperity, in fact, is in large measure due to its liberal commercial policy. If little Holland, without particularly good natural resources of any kind and surrounded by countries with lower wages and standards of living, can prosper under a regime of low tariffs or free trade while most of the world is protectionist, no larger country need have any fears of doing likewise. The notion that it is impossible to pursue a liberal tariff policy in an otherwise protectionist world is quite without foundation. This is clearly demonstrated by the history of British commercial policy. Regardless of reciprocity, any given country could reduce its protective schedules quite as much to its own advantage as to that of other countries.

It is true that a measure of self-sufficiency is automatically imposed on any country, however liberal its commercial policy, as a result of the protective tariffs of others; but this is no reason for an exaggeration of the self-sufficiency by "protective" action on the part of the country so affected. This, as someone has said, is to block up one's own harbors for no better reason than that other people persist in putting obstructions in theirs.[11]

Let us but clearly grasp the facts:

(1) that national prosperity is essentially dependent upon the production of the home popula-

---

[11] The absurd contradiction of efforts to reduce the cost of land and ocean transport, through improvements in railroad or marine engineering, and of simultaneous increases in tariff barriers to keep out goods the import of which is made possible by such improvements, has often been noted. This, however, is only one of many such contradictions.

tion and is not adversely influenced by the competition of foreign countries;

(2) that prices and wages, whether at home or abroad, are, when taken separately, of no relevance to prosperity but that the significant thing is the relationship between them;

(3) that wages can be high relative to prices only as a result of high productivity;

(4) that low wages are a mark of low productivity and, therefore, of rather high money cost of production;

(5) that exports and imports go hand in hand unless, indeed, we give our exports away or receive our imports as gifts from foreign countries, in which case we should be respectively lowering and raising our real incomes;

(6) that buying dear and selling cheap is bad business for a nation as for an individual;

and we shall have banished the illusion that we can be made prosperous by fiat.

It is doubtful whether it is even desirable to attempt to protect good working conditions against sweated foreign competition. A given trade can, of course, be ruined by such competition, but this is impossible for industry in general inasmuch as concentration (abroad) on such an industry involves relative deficiency of output of other products in the countries concerned and therefore a market for the exports of the country with high labor standards.[12] No country need therefore either wait on

---

[12] It will take, of course, only a small volume of exports to pay for the comparatively low priced imports made by sweated labor. Expansion of industries producing for home consumption (or of exports) will therefore tend to accompany the free admission of sweated imports.

others in the adoption of an advanced labor code or protect itself by tariff duties against the products of such countries. Whether it is worth while to protect a given industry against sweated competition raises exactly the same issues as those which center around the question of protection against foreign competition in general. Such protection can be justified only on one or more of the special grounds treated in Chapter V.

An advanced code of working conditions does not influence, in one way or the other, the international *competitive* power of the country in which it is in effect. Such a code may very probably diminish the daily output per worker. If this is not so, competitive power is, *prima facie*, increased.[13] If, however, it is so, and daily output falls, the worker will be exchanging better working conditions for a necessarily lower real daily wage. The price and wage level in the country concerned will sooner or later come into line with foreign prices and wages, as affected respectively by foreign exchange rates and productivity, and it will be no more or less difficult to compete with foreign production than before the adoption of improved working conditions.[14]

---

[13] This situation, however, will not persist since the improvement in productive power will soon be attended with higher real, and probably higher money, wages. *Competitive* power, therefore, will ultimately be unchanged.

[14] If, in the conditions cited, *money* wages are raised, the money will necessarily have less purchasing power and, provided there is no such change in the value of money abroad, will exchange against other currencies on a lower level than before. Real wage, and other, incomes can be paid only out of real output.

The point is pertinent with respect to the program of the National Recovery Administration and agitation for increased duties. There is no logical connection between the policy of raising prices and money wages on the one hand and the desirability of a higher protective tariff on the other. If, by the price-raising policy, the internal value of the dollar is reduced relative to the internal value of other

It is no doubt well worth while to attempt to secure concerted action among different nations in the improvement of working conditions. This is desirable on humanitarian grounds and makes the transition easier for all concerned. Concerted action, however, is by no means necessary, and no country could suffer any permanent injury through adoption, in isolation, of an advanced code of working conditions.[16]

THE PAINS OF TRANSITION

Though protection can now do the United States but little good, and is undoubtedly working harm, the transition to a more liberal policy cannot be painless. The economic structure which has been developed under protection could not survive intact under free trade. It is indeed probable that the transformation, in adjustment

---

currencies, its external value—that is to say, exchange rates—must sooner or later, either automatically or by conscious direction, undergo a substantially equal depreciation. (At the moment of writing the latter is the greater of the two.) In spite of higher dollar prices and costs of production, any given tariff duty tends, therefore, to offer precisely the same protection as it has always done. At the very moment that American producers are claiming that their higher monetary costs require the exclusion of foreign goods, the cry in foreign countries is that the external depreciation of the dollar makes it impossible for enterprisers to compete with their American rivals. The fact is that there is no inherent tendency in the present American policy toward increased national self-sufficiency. If such a movement develops it will be because the proponents of protection will have succeeded in exploiting the popular confusion to their own ends.

[16] The question may be asked why this is true of nations and not true of the plants within any given national industry or of the several sections in any one country. The answer is that national wage levels are automatically adjusted to one another in preservation of international equilibrium, while there is no such adjustment as between plants within an industry or as between the several sections of any one country.

to a liberal commercial policy, would be much less drastic than is ordinarily supposed, since the number and importance of domestically produced transportable products which are substantially dearer in the United States than in foreign countries is not great. There are industries, however, which would suffer severely and a few which might be almost completely eliminated. This is the condition prerequisite to the expansion of those industries in which this country has a comparative as well as absolute competence. No possible good can issue out of a reduction of protective duties except through prior injury to the protected industry.

This is hard doctrine for the Congressman, especially if he happens to come from a district which would be hurt by the removal of protection. It is useless, however, to talk about a more liberal commercial policy unless we are ready to face this fact. Those who urge reduction of duties only where this can be done without any injury to established American industries might as well save their breath. Their proposals, if carried out, would change some rates on the statute books but would have no other effect whatever. If trade is to be made more free some American industries *must* be injured. Such injury is at once the necessary effect of any real lowering of tariff barriers and is the condition of improved foreign purchasing power, the expansion of American export industries, and a more productive specialization in lieu of the less productive Jack-of-all-trades type of economy.

We must make up our minds that we cannot remove a discrimination without damaging those who have been the beneficiaries thereof. We should be serving the public interest both by the abandonment of the discrimination itself and by the improvement in productive powers which we should thereby sooner or later attain, but this cannot be done without cost to vested interests. The cost, however, could be reduced to a minimum if the process were made gradual. By reversing the *trend* of our policy, by moving almost insensibly toward a more liberal regime, by effecting steady reductions in duties over a period of years, we could effect the transition from protection by attrition rather than by violence. The opportunities for profit in export, and in domestic industries not subject to import, would be improved. The capital invested in protected industries subjected to declining profits would not be rendered wholly useless but would not be replaced on as large a scale, if at all, when it wore out. On the other hand, investments of capital in the industries favored by the change in commercial policy would increase. Similarly there would be a gradual transition of labor from the declining to the advancing industries. This would, in the main, be effected by a diversion, away from the declining and toward the growing industries, of workers emerging from adolescence into productive activity. Such diversion of labor and capital would yield nothing but benefits in the development of the comparatively competent at the expense of the comparatively incompetent industries.

The important thing, therefore, is to change the *direction* of commercial policy. Even this is an Herculean task. The injury to established industries will be patent, while the benefits to other industries and to the national economy as a whole, though greater in the long run, will be more or less obscured. It may well be asked, therefore, whether such a change is politically possible. It is certain that any brusque change would be followed by violent reaction. A sudden great lowering of effective duties in the immediate present might well issue in still greater dislocation than is now (1933) prevailing. Since a tariff policy should be determined on long-run considerations only, it is very dubious practice either to raise or to lower tariffs as a cure for business depressions. The depressions issue from maladjustments and there is likelihood that a shift in tariff rates will increase them.

What is needed now is a shift in the national opinion in favor of a more liberal tariff policy to be realized as soon as may be. There should be strong popular opposition to any increase in general tariff schedules. There should, at the same time, be a determination to lower them gradually whenever the business situation is such as to absorb, without undue strain, the immediate shock involved. If schedules are to be lowered there must be a complete abandonment of the pseudo-scientific doctrine of levying tariffs to "equalize costs of production" (equalized delivered costs in domestic markets of duty-paid foreign and of domestic goods).

Nothing could be more ridiculous than the panic which has often been manifested in official circles at the discovery that imports are "invading" our markets at prices below those at which they could be produced in this country. How else could they come in? The very use of the word "invade" is evidence of the psychological perversion which attends discussion of this topic. The vocabulary of war has no place in sound economic thinking, though it has unfortunately found strong lodgment in popular thought. Unless we learn that, in war, one, or more likely both, of the parties must lose, whereas, in specialized production and trade, both parties are likely to gain, we shall go on indefinitely fighting more or less overt trade wars which, like their still more serious political counterpart, are ruinous to all concerned and have even less justification in any sanely conceived social order.

THE DUTY OF CONGRESS

As long as protection is continued it is incumbent upon Congress to justify, to itself at least, a policy of discrimination. In the early days of protection in the United States the issue was clean cut. Rightly or wrongly, the dominant group was of the opinion that it would be well to increase the share of manufacturing industry in our national economic structure and was ready to adopt conscious discrimination to secure this end. The discrimination against the agricultural interest was deeply resented in the South and, up to the time of the Civil War, the struggle for and against protective tariffs on manufactured goods was bitterly waged between the two sections. Success veered now to one side and now to the other. The triumph of the North in the Civil War settled the matter for the time being and, when the South again began to play its proper rôle in the affairs of the nation, it did not speak with one voice.

The situation had changed in two respects. The South was no longer purely agricultural and, in the nation at large, the issue was no longer sharply drawn between agriculture and manufacturing industry. In some lines of agriculture import duties could now give effective protection, while to many lines of manufacture they had ceased to be a benefit and become a burden. The recognition of this fact, however, was slow. The result was complete confusion. The tariff, no longer the means to a very definite end which it could realize, began to be worshiped as an end in itself. It became the palladium of prosperity. Almost every locality had *some* industry which might conceivably benefit through a protective duty, while those who were being harmed were frequently not conscious of the source of their troubles. Advocates of a far-flung protective tariff had a tremendous strategic advantage in the political arena, an advantage which they still possess. It was always possible to point to industries which would be benefited by further protection or ruined by its withdrawal. The benefits were concentrated but the frequently far greater evils had become diffused and therefore obscure.

The result was that the plane of discussion fell to a low level. Alexander Hamilton and his followers, with the definite objective of increasing manufacture at the expense of agriculture, were ready to give the candle for the game and knew exactly why they were discriminating between industries.[16] But who knows nowadays why we so discriminate? Protection of any given industry or group of industries is an understandable policy if, for more or less cogent reasons, that industry or group of industries is desired at the expense of others. But protection for protection's sake is folly.

If our government continues to pursue a policy of interference with the free course of trade, it is at least under the obligation of knowing its objective. It can foster any industry it pleases but only at the expense of other industries and immediately, and probably in the long run also, at the expense of the population at large. It should always have a clear answer to the question why it should favor those industries where protection can be made effective at the expense of those where

---

[16] In Hamilton's day agriculture was relatively so strong as to be able to stand this discrimination without suffering unduly. This is now far from being the case.

it cannot. There will always be industries which "need" protection. This "need" is indubitable evidence of relative incompetence. The real question is whether the country so greatly needs such industries as to be ready to subsidize them at the cost of the population at large and to the detriment of the growth of industries of superior competence.

This question does not turn on having more or less economic activity but on the distribution of our human and material resources so as to produce, on the one hand, more than our consumption of those commodities in which we are specially apt and less of those in which we are not, or, on the other hand, to effect at great expense an equalization in the home production and consumption of each and every commodity. It should always be borne in mind that if we produce more of our own consumption we shall consume more of our own production, that is, we shall cut down on exports.

The answer to the question whether we should produce more or less of our own consumption and, correlatively, consume more or less of our own production, is the answer to the tariff problem. Is foreign trade advantageous? If so, can we have too much of this good thing? And if we can have too much, what is the optimum volume? What goods should we produce at home, and in what proportion to our total consumption? The very consideration of these questions would remove the tariff controversy from the atmosphere of ignorance, prejudice, and special privilege in which it is now immersed, and would force a judgment on specific duties which would have at least some relation to reality and would avoid a solution founded wholly on illusion or on venality.

THE CLARIFICATION OF POLICY

Assuming an attempt at general protection to be abandoned, Congress might more or less rationally seek to protect this or that product in full or in part. It cannot protect all; it cannot protect any except at the expense of others. Instead of imposing upon the Tariff Commission the futile task of finding, if possible, the difference in costs of production of any given commodity at home and abroad,[17] Congress should state an intelligible policy and put upon the Commission the task of finding the rates which will realize the will of the legislature.

Certain commodities, as now, it will no doubt be the will of Congress to admit free of duty or subject to levies for revenue purposes only.[18] Here the appropriate policy is clear and needs no special study. With respect to other commodities, such as sugar, Congress may desire to have part of the domestic consumption produced at home. The decision should then be made either (1) to preserve the present absolute volume of home production, (2) to preserve the present ratio of home production to total consumption, or (3) to so alter conditions as to augment or diminish the absolute or relative share of consumption grown at home. The Tariff Commission might then be given the task of

---

[17] Futile because the object is to levy a duty which will preclude the import of the commodity in question. This result could be obtained without any costly investigation by at once levying a clearly prohibitive duty. Such a duty would have precisely the same effect as if it had been "scientifically" determined.

[18] Such duties would be accompanied by internal excises of equal height wherever, without such excises, they would have a tendency to stimulate home production and thus diminish revenue.

determining the rate which would best carry out the will of Congress thus expressed.

Finally, commodities which Congress deems it best to have domestically produced in the full measure of home consumption offer no difficulties with respect to tariff rates. The rate might be set at almost any level. However high it might be, it could do no more than prevent import; and, provided there is internal competition, the price of the product will be determined by that competition and not by the duty. In case of unconscionable exploitation by a domestic monopoly Congress could set the duty low enough to offer the threat of foreign competition at prices not beyond all reason. Such rates would not be difficult to establish.

If Congress were faced with the task of taking thought on its commercial *policy* rather than on specific rates of duty and if it were moved to consider exactly what proportion of the consumption of any given product it wishes to have produced at home, we might expect more rational action than we now get. If, in the course of time, its experience should clearly show what is in fact the case, that the relative expansion of any industry under the ægis of a protective tariff is accompanied by a corresponding relative contraction of some more competent industry, the urge to pile tariff Ossas on Pelions might perhaps languish. We might even eventually get a recognition of the benefits of a policy of free imports. Until, however, the horror which low-priced imports evoke has been dissipated and until we are ready, in general, to *welcome* imports (at as low a price as they can be obtained) as important contributions to our prosperity, a rational commercial policy is impossible.

Production is only a means to the end of consumption. Protection, in general, represents a bad choice of means to that end. Forgetting that work is but the necessary cost preliminary to the securing of commodities, that it is the commodities, not the work, that we are after, and fallaciously imagining that imports reduce the volume of work "available," we have been led into the supreme folly of making every effort, by export, to rid ourselves of goods (almost regardless of payment as a *national* process),[19] and, by restriction of imports, actually to prevent the acquisition of any *quid pro quo*.[20]

---

[19] Individual exporters, of course, expect payment. But this payment frequently comes indirectly, but none the less truly, from their own compatriots through foreign loans, repayment of which is hindered by the national policy. From the national point of view this is simply giving goods away.

[20] Much of this confusion arises from erroneous notions associated with the "balance of trade" which cannot be better illustrated than by a quotation from Bastiat's "Sophisms."

"A merchant friend of mine having carried through two transactions with vastly differing results, I was curious enough to compare in this matter the accountancy of the counting-house with that of the custom-house, as interpreted by M. Lestiboudois with the sanction of our six hundred legislators.

"Monsieur T. . . dispatched a ship from Havre to the United States, laden with French goods, chiefly those known as *articles de Paris*, amounting to 200,000 francs. This was the figure declared at the custom-house. By the time it arrived at New Orleans the cargo had incurred 10 per cent. charges and paid 30 per cent. duty, bringing the total up to 280,000 francs. It was sold at a profit of 20 per cent., say 40,000 francs, and produced in all 320,000 francs, which the consignee converted into cotton. This cotton had further to bear an additional 10 per cent. for transport, assurance, commission, etc.; so that, on entering Havre, the new cargo amounted to 352,000 francs, and this was the figure entered in the custom-house statement. Finally, Monsieur. . . realised a further 20 per cent. profit on this return cargo, that is, 70,400 francs; in other words, the cotton sold for 422,400 francs.

"If Monsieur Lestiboudois so desires, I will send him an extract from Monsieur T. . .'s books. He will there see set down at the *credit* side of the *profit and loss* account, that is to say as gains, two entries, one of 40,000 francs, the other of 70,400 francs, and

We have retraced the steps toward the self-sufficiency which our forefathers so gladly, and rationally, abandoned. We have long since accomplished the original purpose for which tariffs were levied, and we now retain them, to our own hurt, for no clearly understood purpose whatever. Our modern tariff schedules have been built up in absence of thought on the part of the populace in general but, on the part of the beneficiaries, with an exact knowledge of what they wanted and a sweeping disregard of the interest of the nation at large. It is high time that the national interest were fully considered.

Monsieur T... feels quite sure that his accounts do not mislead him in this matter.

"Yet what do the custom-house returns tell Monsieur Lestiboudois regarding this transaction? They tell him that France has exported to the value of 200,000 francs and imported to the value of 352,000 francs, whence the honourable deputy concludes *'that she has expended and dissipated the profits of her previous economies, that she is marching headlong to ruin, that she has given 152,000 francs of her capital to the foreigner.'*

"Some time later Monsieur T. . . dispatched another vessel, likewise laden with 200,000 francs' worth of the produce of our national industry; but the unhappy ship foundered on leaving port, and nothing remained for Monsieur T. . . to do but to make two little entries in his book, as follows:

"Sundry goods, debtor to X, 200,000 francs for purchase of various articles dispatched by the sailing-ship N.

"Profit and loss, debtor, to sundry goods, 200,000 francs, owing to the definite and total loss of cargo.

"Meantime the custom-house, for its part, made an entry on its records of 200,000 francs exportation; and, as there will never be anything in the way of a corresponding importation entry, it follows that Monsieur Lestiboudois and the Chamber of Deputies will see in this shipwreck a clear net profit of 200,000 francs for France." *Bastiat and the A.B.C. of Free Trade*, translated and edited by Lorenza Garreau, T. Fisher Unwin, Ltd., London, 1926, pp. 109 *et seq.*

APPENDIX I

THE WORLD PRICE SYSTEM IN ITS RELA-
TION TO COMMERCIAL POLICY

It is impossible to deal intelligently with commercial policy without a knowledge of the elementary facts of national and international price structures. These may be laid down in a series of propositions as follows:

Proposition I

Commodity price levels in all countries tend to move into such relationship with one another as will bring about exact equilibrium in the value of the reciprocal transactions of each country with the outside world.

The necessity of paying for imports, and the fact that the only ultimate means of payment is a counter flow of goods and services, forces the price level in every country carrying on foreign trade into such relationship with price levels in the outside world as will lead to an equivalence in value in its total *commercial* exports and imports.[1] The means by which this adjustment of national price levels to one another is reached may be direct, or through exchange rates; but it is, in any case, inevit-

---

[1] See Appendix II for a discussion of financial and non-economic unilateral transactions. These complicate the situation but do not alter the essential principle. *Commercial* exports and imports include commodity and service transactions of a presumptively bilateral character, but exclude, among other things, commodity exports and imports which arise in response to financial transactions involving extended credit.

able.[2] It may be that, in order to secure equilibrium of value of the commercial exports of any given country with its commercial imports, it will be necessary to have the prices of the majority, or, in the opposite case, of but a minority, of its mobile products below the modal price for the commodities concerned. Whatever the persistent deviations of national price levels from one another may be, however, they will be only such as issue from the situation in which the international items of commercial income and outgo show a strict equivalence of value.

Proposition II

Wage rates, and money incomes in general, may vary in any degree from one country to another.

In contrast with the tendency toward an approximation to equality in the various national *mobile commodity* price levels,[3] there is the widest variety of wage, and other, incomes in different countries. The general monetary wage, and other income, levels in any country are, indeed, a function of two variables: (1) the prevailing *world* price level; and (2) the effectiveness of production in the export industries of the country in question.

Apart from minor fluctuations associated with adjustments,

---

[2] Measurement of the various price levels may be made in *any* currency at prevailing rates of exchange. The aberrations of inconvertible paper currency exchange rates from a fairly close equivalence with so-called purchasing power pars are a matter too intricate for treatment in a book of this character. Such aberrations, except in circumstances of an extremely unusual nature, are neither great nor long-continued, and they can be dismissed as of little importance to a discussion of elementary principles. For a detailed exposition of one exceptional case, cf. Frank D. Graham, *Exchange, Prices, and Production in Hyper-Inflation: Germany 1920-1923*, Princeton University Press, Princeton, 1930, Chaps. IV-VI.

[3] The tendency is inevitable only on the condition that there is something like a free market for currencies, the one against the other. If there is no such market, prices in any one country are not comparable with those in another. It is not necessary, however, that the market should be officially recognized. An active "bootleg" market will serve.

price levels in all countries (measured in any currency one cares to take) move up or down together. Money wage levels,[4] *so far as their movement is due to monetary factors,* will also move in sympathy with one another throughout the world, tending to keep the same proportionate relationship, from one nation to another, as before the general sympathetic change in commodity price levels occurred. The more or less constant *relationship* between national wage levels, however (as contrasted with the sympathetic fluctuations in *all* countries), is proportionate to the second of the two variables above mentioned, the effectiveness of production in the export industries of the several countries.[5] Money wages in all export industries in all countries are therefore tied, on the one hand, to the world price structure and, on the other, to respective efficiencies in production. Since differences in monetary return to the export producers of one nation or another are correlated in direct proportion with differences in productive efficiency, money *costs* per unit of output of any commodity tend, of course, to be equal in all countries exporting the commodity in question.

Proposition III

Money wages in the export industries condition money wages in all the other industries of any given country.

Export industries furnish the point of contact with the world price structure. The money wages which, at a given level of world prices for the output of export industries, tend to issue from a given efficiency of production in export lines are communicated by competition to the other industries of the country in question. The equality of money wages which tends to appear

---

[4] *Wage* incomes will here be used elliptically to cover incomes in general.

[5] Competition among workers and employers operates to make this true in the long run for all the export industries whether organized on the basis of a small or large-scale producing unit. In certain cases, however, it may take some years for such competition to exert its full effect, and national monopolies, accompanied by dumping, may occasionally obviate this result altogether.

for all labor of a given grade, in whatever industry it may be employed, is, therefore, at the level which the combination of the existing status of world prices and the efficiency of labor in the export industries permits.

Efficiency of labor in any non-export industry is of no relevance to the money wage obtained therein. Judged by the standard of workers in the export industries, the workers in the non-export industries of any given country may be grossly ineffective in the tasks at which they happen to be employed;[6] they will nevertheless tend to receive the same monetary wage as those of their fellows who are engaged in industries where their effectiveness is high. In such cases relative ineffectiveness will be reflected in high prices for the product of the industries in which it appears.

Only industries *naturally* sheltered, in whole or in part, and export industries will develop in any country under free trading conditions, and they will tend to expand to absorb the whole working population. Under a system of protection, however, any industry, no matter what the price at which its products must be sold in order to cover the high costs per unit of output which issue from relative ineffectiveness, could, if it were worth while, be kept alive. To foster it, however, it is necessary to sacrifice the expansion of some export industry. The acquisition, or maintenance, of the high cost industry is not a matter for congratulation, or its demise a cause for regret.

The higher the effectiveness of naturally or artificially sheltered industries, relative to that of industries producing for export, the lower will sheltered commodity prices tend to be, and the lower, therefore, the general price level in the country concerned. Changes in the relative efficiency of industries producing mobile

---

[6] Such relative efficiencies can be determined only by comparison with the *ratio* of per capita output in the same industries in some other country. Without such a standard of measurement one could never say whether or not any given *per capita* output in any given industry showed an absolute, or even relative, efficiency with that of another industry. The relevant comparison is a comparison between two *ratios*.

goods may at any time lead to the entry of any given industry into the export group and the concurrent elimination of some other industry from that group.[7]

Proposition IV

Differences in individual commodity prices (*not in price levels*) *among the various countries of the world are conditioned by the relative effectiveness of the various industries in each country, absolute effectiveness being irrelevant; differences in* money wages *between countries are conditioned by international differences in absolute effectiveness in common export industries; differences in real wages between countries are conditioned by international differences in absolute effectiveness of industry as a whole.*

Some of the exports of every country are also exports of some other country. Through these common exports wage levels in all countries are linked. In sheltered industries the height of money wages will depend not upon efficiency but upon what workers in the *export* trades can earn. Prices for the output of sheltered

---

[7] While, at any given time, money wages in the export industries may be said to condition money wages in all other industries, it would be wrong to suppose that any fixed group of industries is of more importance than any other group of equal size in the determination of national wage scales. The export industries are such because, at *any* given wage scale, they are the comparatively most competent industries producing mobile goods. Any price and wage structure established in isolation will, on the opening up of international trade, be brought into line with the world price system, and industries will move into or out of the export group according as their comparative competence waxes or wanes. The existing wage scale, coupled with comparative competence, determines the export industries, rather than *vice versa*. All industries employing a given number of workers of a given grade are of equal importance in setting the wage scale for that grade of labor. The point of contact with, and adjustment to, the world price structure is in the export industries, but the relationship between national and world price structures determines what those industries shall be. There is interdependence in the factors.

goods industries must be enough to cover the money wages paid therein.

Real wages are determined by the relation of money wages to prices. Differences in real wages between countries are therefore dependent upon (1) differences of effectiveness in common export trades, which condition the respective money wages in the several countries, and (2) differences in the relative effectiveness, from one country to another, of the sheltered industries, which determine for each country the *prices* of all goods not subject to export or import. Variations in real wages between countries are therefore dependent upon the absolute effectiveness, in each country, of export and sheltered industries taken as a whole.

Proposition V

In international trade, gold is a commodity pure and simple and will move continuously as an export only from those countries in which effectiveness in gold production is high in relation to effectiveness in other industries. In all other gold standard countries gold will move now out of, and now into, any given national area to the extent necessary to bring the national price level into such relationship with the world price structure as will lead to commodity prices below the world level in the relatively effective industries of the said country and above the world level in the relatively ineffective industries.[8] In inconvertible paper standard countries the same result is achieved by shifts in the exchange value of the currency relative to its internal purchasing power.[9]

South Africa offers a case of a country so effective in the production of gold, relative to its effectiveness in other industries, as to be led to rely very heavily on gold exports as a means of

---

[8] High efficiency in any type of export is equivalent to high efficiency in the production of gold, since gold from abroad can be bought, by any country, with other commodities.

[9] In countries with a metallic standard other than gold the case, while analogous, is too complex for treatment here. China is the only important country in this category. Cf. Frank D. Graham, "The Fall in the Value of Silver and its Consequences," *Journal of Political Economy,* Vol. XXXIX, No. 4, p. 425 *et seq.*

payment for imported goods. In commodities other than gold South Africa is likely to be "undersold" by other countries. This is not because South Africa would necessarily be ineffective, in any absolute sense, in the production of many of these commodities, or that money wage rates in South Africa are unduly high. It is simply the necessary condition of the expansion of the relatively effective gold mining industry. For South Africa to be undersold in commodities other than gold is simply the correlative of—indeed, it is identical with—South African underselling of other countries in the commodity gold.

Comment on the latter phases of the present proposition is included in the discussion of Proposition VI.

Proposition VI

The world price system at any given moment is a system of general equilibrium, analogous to the stellar equilibrium, in which every price exerts an influence on every other. Each country tends to produce in excess of its own consumption (and therefore to export) those commodities in which its effectiveness in production is relatively high, and to produce in deficiency of its own consumption (and therefore to import from other countries) those commodities in which its effectiveness in production is relatively low. The export of any given commodity from any country is pushed until the price of the commodity in question falls to the point at which it is equally profitable for that country to export some other (additional) commodity or to concentrate more fully on the home market.[10] The lines dividing the export, domestic, and import commodities of any country move in response to slight changes in the relationship between domestic and world price levels, and these changes are themselves dependent upon the necessity for equilibrium in the country's international accounts. Any industry producing mobile goods may, as a

---

[10] It is perhaps unnecessary to point out that in most countries this happens automatically through the search for profits and the avoidance of losses by individual citizens. The word "country" is used elliptically to mean the citizens thereof.

result of technical changes or changes in reciprocal national de-mands, shift from one of the above categories into another.

In comment on this proposition it will serve to cite a case in which the existing equilibrium in the international accounts of a given gold standard country is not stable but is being maintained by the export of gold taken from bank reserves. The tendency of the export of gold is to lower the domestic and to raise the world price level. Commodities at the time neither exported nor imported (domestic commodities) will feel the full force of the relative lowering of domestic prices, but both export and import commodities will be subject to a dual influence, the one tending to lower and the other to raise prices. Export commodities will tend to fall in price so far as (the home) conditions of supply are dominant and to rise in price so far as (foreign) conditions of demand exert the stronger influence. The opposite is true of import prices. The net effect is likely to be but little change in the prices of the existing exports and imports taken as a whole. Domestic commodities, however, having fallen in price will now enter to some extent into the list of exports; while, since domestic money costs of production will tend to fall with domestic commodity prices, some of the former imports will now be produced in whole, or in larger measure at least, at home. As a result of the high price of the old exports relative to the prices of domestic commodities, a smaller share of such exports will tend to be consumed at home and a larger share will therefore go abroad. The old imports, on the other hand, will to some extent tend to be replaced by the relatively cheapened domestic commodities. Capital and labor will in some measure shift[11] from the production of domestic commodities to the production of more of the old or new exports or of the old imports which are selling at relatively better prices. All of these factors will increase the ratio of commodity exports to commodity imports and thus restore stable equilibrium in the international accounts.

---

[11] There is not likely to be an absolute shift but rather a diversion of new capital in larger measure to the export industries and a failure to replace some of the capital wearing out in the domestic industries.

The same results are obtained under paper currencies through a shift in exchange rates. The somewhat different process is sufficiently explained in the text.

Proposition VII

The dividing lines between exports, domestic commodities, and imports of any given country being established in the manner just stated, money wages for a given grade of labor tend to settle at the figure which, with the whole population employed, represents the money productivity of workers in the export industries under such prices as can be obtained for export products in world markets.

That money wages in the export industries focus money wages in all industries has already been posited. Suppose now that a growth in the working population of a given national unit occurs. The augmentation in the number of workers will be distributed among domestic and export industries in greater or less proportion according as the one or the other type of industry offers a temporarily superior return to labor. The money reward offered will depend on profits, and these will in turn depend on the relative movement of the prices of domestic and export commodities (no change in the relative effort costs of production, or *relative* wage rates, in the two types of industry being assumed). The new, and indeed all, workers must take such *real* wages as they can earn under the new conditions. They can, as a whole, get no more than they produce.[12]

Proposition VIII

Commodity price levels in the various countries, though tending toward substantial equality, will show persistent differences

---

[12] Any increase in the supply of labor and therefore, presumably, of products, is inevitably accompanied by an increase in the "outlet" for products, and therefore for labor to be used in their production. The supply both of labor and of products implies, under anything like a smooth process of adjustment, a correlative demand for labor and for products. This is as true of an improvement in *per capita* output as it is of an increase in the number of workers.

corresponding to the special economic position of each of the countries concerned.

From what has already been said, it will be clear that there is no reason for believing that identity of national commodity price levels would bring the international accounts into equilibrium or, if we look at the interacting phenomena from the other angle, would issue from equilibrium in the international accounts. As far as goods freely exchanged internationally are concerned, national price levels cannot, it is true, depart very far from equality. Prices of sheltered commodities may, however, vary greatly from one country to another.[13] Nevertheless, on the whole, efficiency in the naturally sheltered industries of any given country is not likely to differ in any marked degree from efficiency in the export industries of that country. In fact, *commodity* price levels, therefore, are not likely to differ widely in different countries.[14]

---

[13] Those commodities which are sheltered only by costs of transfer cannot, of course, vary in price from one country to another by more than the amount of such costs. Those, however, which are sheltered by the fact that they are necessarily produced at the point of consumption (roads, railways, houses, retail distribution, personal services, etc.) may vary in price indefinitely, but even these variations are kept within some bounds by the fact that the production of immobile goods requires the use of factors also employed in the production of mobile goods. The price of any given factor of production will, of course, be the same whether it is used in the production of a mobile or immobile finished good, and the relative effectiveness for the one or the other use is not likely to vary in any extreme degree. For a discussion of this topic, *cf.* Bertil Ohlin, *Inter-regional and International Trade*, Harvard University Press, Cambridge, 1933, pp. 141 *et seq.*, a work which seems of outstanding importance in the theory of international trade but which was unfortunately not available at the time of the preparation of the present manuscript.

[14] This statement runs afoul of a popular illusion to the contrary. By anyone, however, who has lived in several different countries, it is likely to be received without much question. The price of *personal services*, of course (and of goods into which service enters in exceptional, degree), tends to be low in poor, and high in rich, countries. This is no more than the inevitable corollary of the general equality of *commodity* prices, since poverty is expressed in

There are, however, certain factors which tend to hold the general commodity price level in certain countries somewhat above, or somewhat below, the modal level for the world as a whole at any given time. The following list of such factors (making for a high, and its converse for a low, national commodity price level), while not intended to be complete, will perhaps be indicative.

(1) The presence of gold mines sufficiently productive to furnish a steady export of gold.

In order to export gold continuously, the commodity price level in the producing country must be high enough to encourage so great a ratio of commodity imports to commodity exports as will compensate the value of the exported gold.

(2) The presence of a large net "unilateral income," or a net income from services, in the international transactions of the country concerned.

Such an income (arising from interest payments in excess of new lending to foreign countries, net receipts from foreign borrowing or from the export of services, net receipts on repaid foreign loans and the like) inevitably leads to an excess of commodity imports over commodity exports. This is induced by a relatively high commodity price level.

(3) A narrow list of exports.

Certain countries, usually small, find it advantageous to concentrate on only a very few commodities for export and to pay for a wide variety of imports with the proceeds of such exports. Since the prices of imports will ordinarily be higher than in the country of origin by the amount of transfer charges involved, and since, in the case under consideration, imports are

---

low money wages, and prosperity in high money wages, with commodity price levels substantially equal. Poverty *might* show itself in not unduly low money wages but in an extremely high price level, and prosperity in very moderate money wages and an extremely low price level; but either of these could occur only in a closed price system and, in the world as it is, this does not happen. There is no evidence whatever for the notion that countries of high wages are countries with a high *commodity* price level, or *vice versa.*

numerous relative to exports, the chances of the general commodity price level being rather high are strong.

(4) Protective tariffs.

Both the reduction of imports and the consequential limitation of exports due to protective duties are associated with an increase in the general commodity price level in the country imposing such duties. The protected goods will obviously tend to sell at higher prices than if they came in free.[15] Gold, being a free import, however, will come into the country to the extent requisite to raise the general commodity price level to the point where exports are eliminated in the degree adequate to compensate the check on commodity imports. Under inconvertible paper monetary standards the same result is achieved through a shift in exchange rates.

(5) Efficiency in a *majority* of non-export industries relatively lower than efficiency in export industries.

This factor has already been adequately discussed.

(6) The presence of national monopoly on a large scale, especially if accompanied by dumping of commodities in foreign markets.

Such monopolies raise prices in the domestic market by restricting supply thereto; and, if a policy of dumping is followed, they lower prices in foreign markets by augmenting the supply which would otherwise be sold therein. The influence on commodity price levels in the several countries is obvious.

(7) High transport costs on imports relative to those on exports.

The higher the transport costs on imports, the greater will be the augmentation of the prices of imports over the prices of those goods in the countries of origin; and the lower the transport costs on exports, the nearer will the prices of exports be to the

---

[15] After protection has been imposed for some years and an efficient industry developed behind the protective barrier, prices of the protected products may indeed fall to the level which would prevail if import were free. If this happens there is no longer any real protection.

relatively high prices on those goods in the countries of destination.

Proposition IX

The absolute height of prices and the absolute height of wages and other money incomes in any given country are, in themselves, of practically no consequence to prosperity. The significant thing is the relationship between them.

Since prosperity is dependent upon commodity prices being low relative to monetary wage and other incomes, high wages with low prices and full employment is the great desideratum. This goal can be achieved only through efficient production; it will be unattainable through attempts to keep money wages in any given country above the level which world prices and the current efficiency of workers in that country prescribe; and it can never be endangered by competition from merely low-wage labor.

Proposition X

The general rate of money wages operative in any country, being proportionate to the effectiveness of labor in the relatively effective export industries, inevitably raises money costs of production in other mobile goods' producing industries in that country above the level prevailing in the same industries in parts of the outside world where such industries are relatively effective.

It makes not the slightest difference how effective industry in general in Country A may be, or how low in B may be the general rate of wages; it will always be impossible for the relatively ineffective industries to meet foreign competition on even terms. The inability to meet foreign prices in these industries is not due to wage or other conditions at home or abroad, or to lack of a rather high degree of absolute efficiency in the industries in question, but to competition for labor from those industries able and willing to pay superior wages though selling in world markets at world prices.

Proposition XI

Export industries do not grow up because of any lack of general consuming power on the part of the home population but because the relationship of the home to the world price structure makes it profitable for domestic entrepreneurs to concentrate, beyond the "requirements" of the home market, in the industries in question, and, ipso facto *therefore, to refrain from entering certain other industries to the extent necessary to provide for the home consumption of the products concerned.*

The consuming ability of a population is neither more nor less than its total production. Whenever, in any country, more of a certain commodity is produced than is consumed at home, it follows, therefore, that less of some other commodity or commodities is being turned out than the home population can and will consume, or lend. This provides the necessary balance of imports with exports.

Export industries arise not because markets at home are limited in any general sense, but merely because it pays to extend such industries rather than build up a productive structure which corresponds, item by item, with home consumption. The notion of the *necessity* of foreign markets as a means of keeping a population employed is wholly illusory and, indeed, silly. Since the exports of one country are the imports of another, such a necessity, if it existed, would mean that it would be possible for any one country to have full employment only by a corresponding volume of unemployment in another. Fortunately this is far from being the case. Rather is it true that full employment in any important country, accompanied by an expansion of both exports and imports, is accompanied by like phenomena in the rest of the world.

To individual entrepreneurs in an industry more than capable of supplying the "requirements" of the domestic market, a foreign outlet for products in general seems essential. But export status in the industry in question was attained solely because there was a better market abroad than at home. This growth was automatically and inevitably paralleled by a better market in the exporting country for certain foreign products to fill the gap which the concentration in export industries necessarily leaves in other lines. The export status for any industry is thus due not to any natural tendency toward expansion beyond the "requirements" of the domestic market but solely to the relationship of the national to the international price structure on the fundamental basis of comparative competence in one line rather than another. When, in response to foreign demand, export status in certain lines has been developed and that demand for some reason then shrinks, the notion arises that expansive forces have been at work which "require" that the export outlet be maintained by hook or crook. The true conclusion, however, is that the shift in demand requires a withdrawal, at least in part, from export status in the industry in question and a development of other export industries or of industries hitherto upon an import basis.

Foreign markets are good only so far as they permit expansion of comparatively competent industries; they ought never to be sought for their own sake, provide no net increase of employment, are automatically accompanied by an equivalent sharing of the domestic market with foreign producers, are not essential to full employment, and are beneficial to all concerned only as they develop in response to the play of prices. Exports and imports are not ends in themselves but means of securing a greater prosperity. Energetic action is good in itself, but if it is devoted to export trade in greater measure than to domestic it is misplaced.[16] The appropriate, most productive, relationship

---

[16] The *volume* of foreign trade is frequently taken as an index of prosperity, but it is of practically no value for this purpose. It is quite possible to have a growing foreign trade while prosperity is declining and an increasing prosperity while foreign trade is shrinking. The discovery of a cheap synthetic process of producing rubber, for instance, would tend to diminish the imports, and therefore the exports, of the United States, though it would enhance our prosperity. A destructive pest, affecting the corn crop so as to put us on an import basis for that product, would, on the other hand,

between foreign and domestic trade will tend to develop naturally if both exports and imports are left free of interference. Such interference can be justified not on the ground of any assumed general necessity but solely on such special grounds as are indicated in Chapter V.

---

tend to increase our total foreign trade, both imports and exports, but would, of course, adversely influence our general prosperity.

APPENDIX II

INTERNATIONAL ECONOMIC TRANSACTIONS AND THE BALANCING OF CLAIMS AND COUNTERCLAIMS

At any given moment some of the residents of any given country will have matured monetary claims upon foreigners while foreigners will, in turn, have matured monetary claims upon the same or other residents of the given country.

If, for example, we take the United States, we shall find that, at any moment, American residents (individual or corporate) will have matured claims against foreigners arising from (1) the sale of commodities, (2) the performance of services, (3) rents and royalties for the use of American-owned property by the foreigners in question, (4) interest, dividends, and profits on investments in foreign securities or businesses, and (5) loans and monetary gifts made by foreigners to Americans. In addition to these private claims, governmental agencies may have matured claims against foreign citizens or governments either for goods and services rendered or as imposts of one or another sort. Foreign private individuals, corporations, or governments would in turn have claims upon American residents or governmental agencies under some or all of the above-mentioned heads.

The monetary claims of residents of the United States on residents[1] of the outside world might be *expressed* either in dol-

---

[1] The word "resident," as employed throughout this discussion, has a rather special meaning associated more closely with the source of accruing income, and the currency in which it is received, than with strictly geographical phenomena. Tourists and other more or

150

lars or in some other money, but, however this might be, the American claimants will normally be finally satisfied only with receipts in dollars. The monetary incomes of the foreign claimees, apart from counterclaims on Americans directly possessed by them, will, however, ordinarily accrue in some other currency. In order that the payments may be made, an exchange of other currencies against the dollar will be necessary. The American claimants will either sell foreign currencies for dollars (buy dollars with foreign currencies) or the foreign claimees will do the same thing. The form of transfer depends on whether the American claimant draws on the foreign claimee or the latter remits to the American. The situation of the claimants in the United States is, of course, paralleled in every other country. Foreigners who have claims against American residents will, in consequence, either sell dollars for their own currency (buy their own currency with dollars) or the American claimees will take the initiative in a similar transaction.

Since international economic transactions are typically, and under normal conditions, all but universally, carried on by

less permanent expatriates, who are deriving their monetary income from a country other than that in which they are sojourning, are to be regarded as residents of the country from which their monetary income derives rather than of that in which they are at the moment living. For purposes of international accounting the goods and services bought and consumed *in situ* by such more or less temporary expatriates are as truly exports of the country of sale, and imports of the country of "residence," as if they had been delivered across the respective national boundaries. On similar principles goods sent from the country of residence to the country of sojourn, for the use and account of an expatriate "resident" who pays for them out of funds accruing to him in his country of residence, are not to be counted as exports, or, if so counted, should be balanced by some such item as "Reduction in the home monetary holdings of residents sojourning abroad effected in payment for exports." *Services* rendered in one country to residents of another who are on home territory are, however, to be regarded as on a par with an actual transfer of commodities. The service can, in this case, be held to have crossed the frontier as one side of a bilateral transaction for which money or its equivalent, crossing the border in the opposite direction, is the *quid pro quo*.

freely contracting, profit-seeking, private individuals or corporations who quite rightly take no thought of equilibrium in the international accounts, it is clear that the cash claims of residents of any one country against the foreign world may at any given moment tend to exceed or to fall short of claims in the opposite direction. It would, indeed, be miraculous if they did not. As far as claims and counter claims offset one another, however, those residents of any one country who have claims on foreigners may sell their claims on foreign currency to those of their own nationals who have obligations to meet in the foreign currency in question. The latter can then transmit these claims to their foreign payees who will collect in their own currency from those of their own nationals against whom the claims apply.

It is the business of exchange dealers in any country to bring together the two groups of citizens of that country who have respectively claims against, and obligations to meet in, some other currency, and to offer them the opportunity to buy and sell such claims in their own currency. When, however, in any country, the existing matured claims to foreign currencies exceed or fall short of matured counter claims on the domestic currency, some of the parties concerned would, *in the absence of some adjustment of claims or of some supplementary means of payment*, be unable, in the one case, to convert into their own currency their claims to foreign money or, in the other, to make payment to foreign claimants in the requisite currency.[2] *Equilibrium in the international accounts is consequently essen-*

---

[2] Though, for reasons presently to be adduced, it is normal for the *total* claims to foreign currencies of the citizens of any given country to balance the *total* foreign claims to the currency of the country in question, it is most unlikely that the claims of the citizens of any one country on any single foreign currency will balance the counter claims of payees desiring that particular currency. But, since any currency with an international market can be freely exchanged for any other, no difficulty arises on this score. The desired foreign currency can be bought either directly with the domestic or with some other money which has first been acquired with domestic currency, commodities, services, or the like.

tial to this ordinary settlement of international claims taken as a whole.

Since an excess of claims to foreign currencies over foreign claims in the opposite direction implies, in its obverse aspect, a corresponding deficit, it will be sufficient to consider the effects either of an excess, or a deficit, of claims to foreign currencies in relation to the foreign counter claims to the currency of any given country. Whatever happens in a country which has an excess of claims to foreign countries is simply the obverse of what happens in some other country which has a deficit, and *vice versa*. Let us therefore take as an illustration a case in which Americans have claims to foreign currencies in excess of the foreign claims to dollars.[8]

If, at a given status of rates of exchange between dollars and foreign currencies, the cash claims of Americans against foreign currencies should exceed foreign cash claims to dollars, the excess of the offer of foreign currencies in exchange for dollars over the offer of dollars for foreign currencies would lower the dollar value of the foreign currencies or, what is the same thing, would raise the foreign currency value of the dollar. So far as the American claims on foreigners were expressed in foreign currencies rather than in dollars, their dollar value would sink automatically with the shift in exchange rates, and the foreign parties under obligation to make payment on these claims would be able to extinguish them with fewer dollars than would otherwise be necessary.

If, at the same time, foreign claims on Americans were expressed in dollars, the amount of dollars immediately available to foreign demanders would, of course, be unaffected. A change in the rate of exchange might thus so alter the relative value of reciprocal obligations in any one currency as in itself to eliminate the disequilibrium which originated the movement in the rate.

---

[8] The only claims in question here, as elsewhere in this discussion, are those which their holders are desirous of converting *immediately* into their own currency. They are matured claims which their holders intend to cash.

It might happen, however, that American claims on foreigners were predominantly expressed in dollars, and foreign claims on Americans predominantly in foreign currencies, and in this case the assumed movement of exchange rates would augment the disequilibrium and would therefore be self-accelerating rather than self-limiting. The currencies in which international obligations tend to be expressed are a matter of varying trade practice, and no rule can be laid down as to the probability of one of the above results rather than the other.

In all but highly pathological cases, however,[4] it is a matter of comparative indifference whether the tendency of a movement in exchange rates is, in itself, to increase or to diminish the disparity between claims and counterclaims. This is because the disequilibrium between the American offer of foreign currencies and the foreign offer of dollars,[5] at the hitherto prevailing exchange rates, will, in normal circumstances, always be reduced by the new dollar demand for foreign currencies which will appear as the dollar prices of those currencies fall, and by the concurrent decrease in the foreign currency demand for dollars on the part of all foreign seekers of dollars who can defer their purchases of that currency.

The disequilibrium will not only be reduced but it will be eliminated, either by a sufficient fall in the dollar value of foreign currencies or, if such a fall is necessarily confined within narrow limits by the presence of a gold standard in the countries concerned, by the substitution of direct payments to Americans in gold in lieu of payments in dollar exchange. In both cases the necessary supplementary means of payment are evoked by the movement of exchange rates. Under normal circum-

---

[4] Such as prevailed in Germany from the end of the World War to late 1923.

[5] It is immaterial whether the situation is expressed in terms of offer (supply) or of demand. An American offer of foreign currencies is but the obverse of a foreign currency demand for dollars, and a foreign offer of dollars the obverse of an American demand for foreign currencies. We may therefore speak either of reciprocal demand, or of reciprocal supply, as covering the whole situation.

stances, even with a paper standard, no very large movement in exchange rates will be necessary to this end.

There is at all moments, therefore, exact equilibrium between the dollar (or any other) demand for foreign currencies and the foreign currency demand for dollars (or any other money), the movement of exchange rates or the transfer of gold being the equilibrator. There can, at most, be but a *tendency* toward disequilibrium which may be recurrent or, for a time, continuous, but is always counteracted by a shift in the rate of exchange of one currency against another to the degree necessary to provoke at least temporary equilibrium.

Since time is but a succession of moments, this series of momentary equilibria stretches out into a permanent moving equilibrium. *The exchange equilibrium prevailing at any moment may be stable or unstable.* If, for instance, the accruing cash claims of Americans against foreigners show a continuous tendency to exceed the foreign counter claims on American dollars at the gold export point for foreign gold currencies or at the rate of exchange momentarily in effect on free currencies, the equilibrium temporarily attained will be unstable. Under these circumstances dollar exchange rates will show a persistent upward tendency or gold will continue to flow to the United States from such foreign gold standard countries as have an insufficient accrual of claims to dollars (and other foreign currencies) to effect a balance with accruing American (and other extra-national) claims to their respective currencies, until a stable equilibrium is achieved either on the gold basis or on the inconvertible paper basis to which such countries may be forced. In the latter case, as in the case of all countries originally possessed of such a free currency standard, the dollar value of the currency concerned will fall until the requisite stable equilibrium is attained.

For a time, it is true, a quasi-permanent equilibrium may result from the extension of short-term loans (including all other than sight bills of exchange) by which the residents of countries having an excess of claims against foreign money furnish the residents of countries where the opposite conditions prevail with the requisite supply of the scarcer currency. But this only palliates, it does not cure, the situation, since such loans soon have to be paid back. A more lasting equilibrium may issue from a similar extension of various types of long-term loans,[6] especially if this takes on a steadily cumulative aspect. Such loans may be a perennial factor in the establishment of what, in such situations, must be regarded as a fairly stable long-term equilibrium. But even in these circumstances mounting interest payments will sooner or later compel more fundamental adjustments which will be initiated by movements of exchange rates along the lines already indicated. In any event there is no escape for any nation, in the long run, from a position of stable equilibrium in its international accounts, a position in which, with a stable rate of exchange and no abnormal movement of gold across its borders, the claims to foreign currencies steadily accruing to its nationals are exactly balanced by the claims to its own currency steadily accruing to foreigners.[7]

The sustained augmentation of accruing claims to foreign currencies relative to accruing foreign claims to the domestic currency which occurs as a corrective after a country has suffered an adverse movement in exchange rates, or a drain of gold, ordinarily issues from the resulting shift in relative prices in the country in question and in the outside world.

In the case of gold standards, a country which is persistently losing gold from its bank reserves, or from circulation, *must* get its price level down relative to that of the outside world, if it is not to be forced sooner or later to abandon its chosen standard and adopt an inconvertible paper currency.[8] When relative price

---

[6] Short loans, or a reservoir of them, constantly renewed, become, for purposes of international balances, loans at long term.

[7] Claims by foreigners may be canceled or commuted by bankruptcy, repudiation, or the refusal of the authorities of the debtor country to permit the purchase of the foreign exchange necessary to their payment. This is one way to secure equilibrium but, needless to say, it does not facilitate future adjustments through the borrowing process.

[8] The loss of gold, of course, is itself a strong stimulus toward the reduction of credit and convertible paper currency in the coun-

levels are sufficiently altered, the resulting relative increase in foreign buying in the country of comparatively lowered prices, and the relative decrease in the purchases of citizens of that country in countries of comparatively higher prices abroad, will bring about the requisite equilibrium in accruing foreign claims and counter claims.[9]

In the case of inconvertible paper monetary standards, whether originally in force or later voluntarily or involuntarily adopted, the inevitable fall in the exchange value of the currency of any country on which foreign cash claims are in excess of the domestic cash claims to foreign monies will, of itself, lower the foreign currency price of all commodities and services in the country in question and will, conversely, increase the domestic currency price of all foreign commodities and services. The result is the same as under gold standards.

Under gold standards, exchange rates are all but absolutely fixed, and adjustment takes place through a shift in relative prices in the various countries. Under free currency standards, on the other hand, it is rather prices which take on a fixed character,[10] and adjustment takes place through a shift in ex-

---

try in question, and this is the mechanism which is ordinarily relied upon for a lowering of the price level. But, to take a recent case, this was an insufficient stimulus, or the process could not be effected rapidly enough in Great Britain in 1931, with the abandonment of the gold standard as a necessary result.

* The mere diminution in monetary incomes in a country which has been subjected to contraction in its money supply will tend toward smaller purchases, at given prices, of all kinds of goods, both those produced domestically and those imported. More domestic commodities will therefore be available for export and will be exported in response to the relatively good marketing opportunities which will then be open in foreign countries. The requisite expansion of commodity exports, relative to imports, of the country in question may thus be attained, through a movement in opposite directions in both categories of foreign trade, without any significant change in relative national price levels having first taken place.

[10] Price levels in paper standard countries are, of course, by no means absolutely fixed. *But the domestic price level is not necessarily much altered, as gold prices in any given country tend to be, by the status of the international accounts.* It is much more within the

change rates. In the case of gold, paper, or any other monetary standard, there will be no surcease from a movement of the metal (with accompanying changes in the relationship between prices in the several countries concerned) or, in the alternative, a progressive shift in exchange rates in a given direction, until a stable equality between the accruing claims and counter claims on any and all currencies is attained. Such a stable equilibrium is of course but a norm around which there are constant minor fluctuations, largely canceling one another, but it is the condition to which there is always an irresistible tendency to return whenever any deviation therefrom happens to occur. It is indeed the condition indispensable to national solvency; and national solvency, if not voluntarily assumed, is in the long run imposed from outside by the impossibility of obtaining imports.

If immediate claims and counter claims with respect to the currency of any given country show a persistent adverse tendency, an (unstable) equilibrium will nevertheless be attained from day to day by means of (1) the export of gold from bank reserves or circulation, (2) a shift in exchange rates which brings about the circumstances noted on page 154, (3) short-term loans, either voluntary or involuntary,[11] (4) the cancellation or commutation of some of the claims through bankruptcy of the obligor, restrictions on payment imposed by his government, or more or less voluntary gift on the part of the payee, or (5) the lifting of some of the claims through a long-term loan.

Long-term loans, in appropriate circumstances, may be a more or less continuous and healthy phenomenon. But no one will in-

---

volition of the monetary authorities. If the price level is shifting at the same time that exchange rates are moving as a result of unstable equilibrium in the international accounts, the exchange rates must eventually settle at a level which will take into account the change in relative prices in the various countries *as well* as bring stable equilibrium into the international accounts. Under paper standards adjustment of the international accounts can be left to the movement of exchange rates; under gold standards it necessarily involves internal price levels whenever disequilibrium is great.

[11] An involuntary loan arises when a debtor arbitrarily postpones a payment which is due.

definitely continue to make long-term loans to the residents of any country merely for the purpose of postponing the incidence of immediate obligations on such persons or their compatriots. That way lies disaster.[12] If, and when, the disaster occurs (and it frequently issues from a refusal on the part of lenders to take further risks), many maturing claims are wiped out by default or by bankruptcy, and a healthy, if disillusioned, situation develops in which no country lives in an inevitably temporary luxury far beyond its means and at the expense of unwary foreign investors. All the other means of securing temporary equilibrium are at least as quickly exhaustible as are the resources from *ad hoc* long-term loans.

When such emergency resources are exhausted, a stable equilibrium is automatically established by a downward movement of the exchange value of the currency of the country in question to the point which will restrict purchases abroad to a value no more than the accruing value of claims on foreign currencies. The only means for preventing the exhaustion of emergency resources, once there is a tendency toward an excess of foreign claims over domestic counter claims to the respective currencies, is the reduction of the national price level, relative to price levels in other countries, to a figure which will provide a stable equilibrium without drawing further upon any of the emergency resources above noted. This reduction in the price level will tend to be absolute under gold standard conditions while, under paper standards, it may be merely relative to the rise in foreign exchange rates.

Apart from cancellation of claims through bankruptcy and the like, the total maturing claims of the residents of any given country upon foreigners must therefore continuously meet the counter claims of foreigners against residents of that country, and *vice versa*; and the movement of relative national price

---

[12] Such disasters are by no means rare; we are, at the moment of writing, passing through a period in which the process just described has resulted in numerous defaults on long-term obligations. Such happenings, however, put an effective quietus on the process from which they issue.

levels, or of exchange rates, is the principal mechanism by which permanent equilibrium is achieved. The forces involved are as inevitable in their operation as is the motion of the stars; and no effort permanently to raise the total of accruing claims on foreigners over the total of accruing foreign claims on the nationals of any country can result in anything but frustration. The claims may indeed be acquired but they can never be cashed. A country seeking continuously to acquire claims on foreigners in excess of foreign counter claims on its own nationals is, in the degree in which it attains its aim, therefore quite sure of mulcting itself.

This is why it is the height of folly to go on year after year in a blind policy of stimulation of exports and restriction of imports. This can be done with some success as long as claims are postponed through the lending process, but it cannot be done indefinitely without making repayment of the loans impossible. Carried far enough, it renders even interest payments impossible except in a crescendo of new borrowing and lending. Whatever the volume of loans, an exact balance of realizable claims and counter claims, including those arising from past and present capital transactions, is inevitable, and equilibrium will be achieved by way of bankruptcy if other roads are closed.[18]

However slow legislatures may be in apprehending this fact, it has, in administrative circles, been more and more fully recognized in recent years. The Department of Commerce of the United States, for instance, has for about a decade been publishing an annual account of the international payments of the United States in which an attempt is made to assess all international economic transactions to which residents of the United States, or the American government, have been a party in the year in question. The account for the year 1930 is reproduced, with some changes in grouping, on page 168. The Department has itself expressed dissatisfaction with some of the items in this

---

[18] Fortunately for mercantilistically inclined nations, automatic forces *tend* to produce this result without bankruptcy, in spite of all efforts to prevent it by misguided commercial policies.

account, but though the approximate balance stated may be, in some degree, meretricious, this is due to errors in the statistics. There is no disposition to question the fact that equality in the two sides must be, and was in fact, achieved.

In any given year the *matured* claims arising out of present or past long-term loans or other capital charges (claims of the borrowers or recipients in the one case and of receivers of interest, of repayments of principal, and of tribute in the other), as well as gifts, must of course be included in the balance sheet since they give to the borrowing countries, or to the countries receiving interest, repaid principal, tribute, or gift precisely the same immediate claims to other currencies as would have arisen out of the export from the recipient countries of a volume of commodities, over and above that actually sent, equivalent in value respectively to the loans, the interest, the repaid principal, the tribute or the gift.[14] *Deferred* claims, arising out of long-term loans or other capital charges (claims which will accrue to the lenders as interest and repayment of principal only in years to come), are, on the other hand, not included.

The international balance of payments for any given period (usually a certain year) shows only the claims actually matured

---

[14] The *immediate* position of a borrower from abroad is precisely the same as that of an exporter or of a receiver from abroad of interest, repaid principal, gift, or tribute. All have immediate claims on foreign currencies. The *immediate* position of a lender on foreign account, on the other hand, is precisely the same as that of an importer, a payer of interest, of the principal on an old loan, of tribute, or of the donor of a gift to residents of foreign countries. All are subject to immediate claims on their currency *by* foreigners and may be called claimees. For this reason the words "debtor" and "creditor," or "debit" and "credit," as used in international accounts, are very confusing. They are therefore not used in this book. The international balance sheet deals with present transactions only. The lender, whom we are accustomed, in looking at the future rather than the present, to call the creditor, is, in the first instance, a claimee under an immediate duty to turn money over to the foreign borrower. He is, therefore, at the moment a debtor on international account. Similarly, a borrower *is*, in the *first instance*, a *creditor* on international account.

in that period. It is the international *cash* account. It deals, in consequence, with international financial items only so far as these have given rise to cash claims during the period covered by the statement. The general *status* of any country as an international lender or borrower, the "statement of condition,"[15] could be determined only by far-fetched implication from the statement of cash claims and counter claims. To show clearly the status and trend of international capital assets and liabilities, it would be necessary to have a quite different type of account dealing solely with international investment and other accumulations of deferred claims and not at all with trade, service, and even financial, items of a *current* character. With this type of account we shall have little to do in this book, since the matters with which it deals are, at most, ancillary to the purpose in hand.

The ordinary *Balance of Payments* statement shows only such transactions as were actually consummated (either completely or unilaterally) in the period to which it refers, and it is with these that we are primarily concerned. The statement of the *international financial status* of any given country would show, on the other hand, a mass of future claims and counter claims which will not become of importance in the international balance of payments until they mature. Financial items appear in the balance of international payments only as maturities, *i. e.*, whenever a payment is *due*. This may be the transfer of the original principal of a loan, amortization of an existing obligation, interest, or any other payment. Such items would appear

---

[15] It is somewhat misleading to develop analogies between the accounting of private business and that of international trade. The end of a private business is monetary profit and this monetary profit is turned over to the owners. But the international accounts include both the transactions of businesses, as such, and of the owners thereof. Just as the earnings of a corporation are a debt to its stockholders and the two items as debit and credit cancel out, so it is with a country in its international accounts. The aim of international transactions is not, or should not be, a national *monetary* influx, but improvement in national economic welfare. Profit can be made without any change in the national supply of money.

in the *Statement of Condition*, on the other hand, only when they are *not* due but were simply the estimated present worth of rights to future income or the as yet unmatured obligations from which these rights take their substance. These rights and obligations may have been acquired or assumed in exchange for a past *quid pro quo*, or they may have been acquired or assumed by way of tribute. The significant thing is that they do not impose any *present* payments on anyone.

Since Balance of Payments accounts are concerned only with matured items, it usually makes little difference whether or not capital transactions are separated from the others. Capital (credit) transactions in the international balance of payments are, however, a complicating factor to which attention must now be given. Their significance will be better grasped after an analysis of some characteristic features of such items.

The volume of long-term international loans made in any year by any one of the great lending countries ordinarily far exceeds the net outward movement of gold, if any, from the lending country in question. Similarly, the great borrowing countries do not ordinarily receive any great influx of gold. The loans are therefore almost entirely consummated in exported and imported goods or services other than gold, though the goods are usually exported, or the services performed, not by the individual lenders but by some of their compatriots to whom the lenders, on order of the borrowers or of assignees of the latter, turn over the borrowed sums. Similarly, the individual borrowers do not themselves necessarily, or even ordinarily, import goods or services, but sell their claims to others who have made, or wish to make, such imports.

The actual purchase of foreign securities is, indeed, from the economic as contrasted with the financial point of view, merely an *undertaking* to make a foreign loan, and is not by any means its full immediate consummation. The loan is not economically consummated until an equivalent value of goods is sent, or services performed, by residents of the lending to or for residents of the borrowing country or to residents of some other country to whom the borrowers have assigned their claims. The loan is therefore *really* made in commodity exports, or in services performed for foreigners, by residents of the lending country. The only immediate compensation for such commodity or service exports is a written promise, or a mere unexpressed hope,[16] of future tangible receipts which the investors can eventually realize only through direct commodity imports,[17] the purchase of goods or services in the country of investment, or the sale of their foreign currency receipts to such of their own countrymen as wish thus to import commodities or pay for goods or services rendered them abroad. Interest can, in fact, be paid only in the way in which the loan can only be really made. If, early in its history, the investment is defaulted or otherwise fails, there will never be any real compensation for the real commodities exported, or the services performed, at the time that the loan was made. On the other hand, if the investment continues to yield interest or dividends over a long period of years, the real commodities exported or services performed, in payment of interest, by citizens of the borrowing country will eventually mount up to a much greater total value than the value of commodities or services exported from the lending country at the time the loan was made.

Interest, in whatever form received, might perhaps be regarded as the payment for the service of continuous refrainment by the lender from the consumptive use of his property. We sometimes, indeed, speak of interest payments as payments of "service" on the loan. For this service, as it is rendered, immediate payment is due. Interest payments, thus considered, are on a par with payments for any other present service or for commodities.

The case is necessarily different, however, with loans and investments. The loan or investment itself is an obvious service rendered to the borrower, or country of investment, by the

---

[16] Such as the hope of profits from a direct investment in, let us say, the building of a factory on foreign soil.

[17] Including, perhaps, a small amount of gold.

lender. For this service, however, no immediate payment is made by the recipient, individual or country, but only an express or implied promise or prospect of payment at a later date is given. In the case of fixed interest securities, which may be taken as typical, the loan gives to residents of the borrowing country claims against the currency of the lending country which are acquired without the present export of any commodity or the present performance of any service as a *quid pro quo*. The value of the present exports of goods or services, *by* residents of the lending country, will therefore exceed the value of the present imports of goods or services *for* residents of the lending country, by the full amount of the loan. The contrary will, of course, be true of the borrowing country. So far as international transactions include net borrowing there can thus be no real present balance of values in international outgo and receipt of goods plus services, and an accounting balance can be secured only by including the item of loans and investments in the international cash balance sheets as if such loans and investments were a commodity or service export of the borrowing, and import of the lending, country.

A casuist might assert that the receipt of the proceeds of an international loan is the present payment for a present export of *promises* or *prospects of profit* (securities or the hope of future earnings). It seems better, however, frankly to recognize the fact that, where loans are concerned, no present balance in the value of exported and imported commodities and services occurs. The same is true, of course, in the opposite direction, where repayment of a loan is made or foreign property is sold. Moreover, so far as international loans are never repaid,[18] and so far

---

[18] Loans, in the sense of the word as here used, necessarily include the more or less slowly changing *total* of book accounts and such similar items as are secured by promissory notes, bills of exchange, or any other form of credit. The growth of the total of foreign investment means, in effect, that there is an increasing volume of international indebtedness never repaid. The *reservoir* of short-term indebtedness, however rapid the shift in individual items, is equivalent to a loan of the *in perpetuum* type.

as voluntary gifts or tribute enter the picture,[19] a real balance in the values of international outlay and receipt of goods and services by any given country is no more attained in the long run than it is in the immediate present.

Whether interest payments should or should not be put in the same category with the principal of loans and with gifts, depends upon whether interest is to be regarded as a payment for present or past services. As has been indicated above, it is theoretically more appropriate, perhaps, to regard interest payments as the return for the service of continuous abstention on the part of the lender from the consumptive use of his property—the rental for the service of leaving that property in the hands of the borrower—than as the return for the original transfer of the capital.[20] Since, however, services of this sort can be rendered without present labor cost, in the sense that the provision of this service in no wise forestalls other productive activity on the part of the lender or requires that he give any current *quid pro quo* in the form of concrete goods or active effort for the interest payments received, it is, for some purposes, more useful to classify interest payments along with principal on capital account and other unilateral items. This has been done in the table on pages 168 and 169.

In the construction of international balance of payments accounting sheets the logical issue of the discussion in the preceding pages is a distinction between (1) bilateral transactions, in which for every individual item and as between the parties directly concerned, there is, within the accounting period, a pre-

---

[19] The items "Loans" and "Gifts" are, as noted above, ordinarily entered in international cash balance sheets as if they were payments, *by the recipients*, and receipts, *by the donors*, of some *quid pro quo* for the goods, money, or services by means of which the loans or gifts are actually consummated. This achieves an accounting balance but it hardly squares with reality. There is no present, and there may *never* be any, economic *quid pro quo*.

[20] The appropriate return for such original transfer is the repayment of principal. The view of interest here taken encounters difficulties when the annual payments are in the form not of contract interest but of dividends or profit on direct investment of capital. The view presently to be adduced may therefore be preferable.

sumptive *quid pro quo*,[21] and (2) unilateral transactions for which, as between the parties directly concerned, there is, within the accounting period and perhaps in perpetuity, no such presumptive *quid pro quo*. As far as *contractual* transactions are concerned, this division will mean simply a separation of cash[22] and capital (credit) items, but the unilateral transactions will also include those which are permanently, as well as currently, one-sided.

The bilateral transactions are merely *presumptively* such, even as between the parties directly concerned, since any given item in the accounts, *e.g.*, merchandise exports, may contain goods which have been sent direct to a resident of foreign countries as a gratuitous remittance from a friend or relative in the sending country. Any net balance on the unilateral transactions must, in fact, be covered by a like balance, on the opposite side, in the transactions *presumptively* bilateral. The great bulk of the *presumptively* bilateral transactions, however, are, as between the individuals directly concerned, *really* bilateral though any one of the individuals in question may have obtained the *quid pro quo* which he offers in a trading transaction through a prior purchase, with his own currency, of a claim on a foreign currency arising from some unilateral transaction. If the unilateral international monetary transactions of the United States should be all in the one direction—giving claims to residents of foreign countries on American currency—the ostensibly bilateral transactions would, with exact accounting, necessarily show an excess of American claims on residents of foreign countries, over the corresponding counter claims of residents of foreign countries on Americans, equal to the total claims of foreigners in the unilateral category. As a matter of fact, in the table as given, United States' residents showed a small deficit of claims as against counter claims on bilateral transactions and, at the same time, a similar deficit on both contractual and non-contractual

---

[21] Either in goods, services, or money. The transaction may involve an exchange of goods (including services) for money, of goods for goods, or money for money.

[22] Including short-term credit charges incurred and paid off within the accounting period.

UNITED STATES

ESTIMATED BALANCE OF INTERNATIONAL PAYMENTS IN TERMS
OF DOLLARS

(Hypothetical year)[21]

American Residents in Account with Foreign Residents	Claims	Counter Claims
Items from which Reciprocal Claims upon Foreign and on United States Currencies Arise	Matured Claims of American Residents on Persons Residing Abroad (Millions of Dollars)	Matured Claims of Foreign Residents on Persons Residing in the United States (Millions of Dollars)
I. Bilateral Transactions (involving a presumptive current *quid pro quo*)		
1. Merchandise (ordinary exports and imports)...............	3843	3061
2. Gold, silver, and currency[a].....	216	461
3. Freight charges................	155	251
4. Tourist expenditures..........	206	811
5. Bunker coal and oil...........	44	10
6. Ship chandling, ship repairs, etc.	46	31
7. Vessels sold..................	3	3
8. Parcel post shipments (so far as otherwise unrecorded).......	18	—
9. Sales of electric power, advertising, cablegram and telephone charges, underwriters' commissions, etc.	53	62
10. Adjustments, for differences in year-end lags, etc.	—	59
Total Bilateral Transactions	4584	4749
II. Unilateral Transactions (involving no presumptive current *quid pro quo*)		
a) Contractual		
1. Capital investment transactions (including direct investment, international transfer of existing securities, refunding, and repayment)..................	2249	2567
2. Earnings of long-term private investments..............	838	227

U. S. BALANCE OF PAYMENTS—*Continued*

American Residents in Account with Foreign Residents	Claims	Counter Claims
3. Earnings of short-term private investments..........	78	73
4. Motion picture royalties.....	90	6
5. Patent and copyright royalties, etc.	15	15
6. Insurance transactions......	70	70
7. Net change in international banking accounts[b].......	—	485
Total Contractual Unilateral Transactions	3340	3443
b) Non-contractual		
1. Migrants' contributions.....	33	199
2. Missionary and charitable contributions............	—	49
3. War-debt payments........	241	—
4. Other inter-governmental payments...............	46	127
Total Non-contractual Unilateral Transactions	320	375
III. Adjustment for errors and omissions[c]	323	—
GRAND TOTAL (all items)	8567	8567

[a] This includes gold earmarked for foreign account or taken out of earmark. When gold is earmarked for foreign account it is to be construed as exported and when taken out of earmark it is to be construed as imported.

[b] Only the net change is here given since figures are not available for the transactions in detail. Everything outside of the net figures represents, of course, a cancellation, within the period, of claims and counter claims.

[c] Rigid precision is impossible in estimates such as these; but in addition to inevitable error in the figures it should be remembered that the items are all translated into dollars. Any item may, however, accrue in dollars or in any other currency. Shifts in exchange rates between the date of contracting and paying obligations (though both occur within the accounting year) may, therefore, cancel a part of, or enlarge, the obligation as measured in dollars. Such changes might easily account for the whole of the item here included under errors and omissions. If obligations expressed in foreign gold currencies were translated in the year in question into gold dollars at par, some error must arise as a result of deviations of the actual exchange rates from parity. There may also be certain "involuntary" loans arising from a failure to secure payment when it is due. These involuntary loans would not ordinarily appear as loans in the official statistics, which would assume their payment, and the accounts would then fail to balance by this amount.

[23] Cf. *The Balance of International Payments of the United States,* Government Printing Office, Washington, (yearly).

unilateral account. Errors and omissions somewhere must be responsible for this anomaly, and the deficit on all three accounts of course adds up to the total of such errors for which allowance is made.

If perfect accuracy could be attained, the difference between presumptive bilateral claims and counter claims would show exactly the difference between the value of goods and services *currently* given and of goods and services currently received by the United States in its international dealings. The same could, of course, be said of the difference between the unilateral transactions, the excess or deficit of claims over counter claims acquired on the one account balancing the deficit or excess of claims over counter claims acquired on the other. The net national balance of unilateral claims is met by a corresponding net balance of bilateral claims in the opposite direction. Loans, interest, etc., are paid in goods and, in the Balance of Payments, involve duplication. This is necessary to achieve an accounting balance.

Though there is thus no necessary equivalence between the total value of present commodity and service exports and the total value of present commodity and service imports and, so far as total foreign investment grows or goods are voluntarily or involuntarily given away,[24] no equivalence even in the long run, there is nevertheless a close sympathetic relationship between commodity and service exports and imports.

The items entering at any time into the international economic accounts may conveniently be classified as (1) fixed, (2) independently variable, and (3) appropriately elastic, that is, varying in such a way in response to a disturbance as to produce a new equilibrium.

The fixed items are those arising out of maturing unconditional obligations to pay a given amount of a given currency on which no default is made. The best example is interest on honored bonds though all maturing obligations to pay a definite amount of money are, if met, in this category. Fixed items, unless eliminated by bankruptcy or the like, cannot, of course,

---

[24] On one of the interpretations above given this is also true of interest payments.

respond in adjustment of any tendency toward disequilibrium in the international balance of payments.

Any variable item, on the other hand, obviously *might* respond in the direction required to adjust a tendency toward disequilibrium. If, however, the variability is independent of the results of such a tendency, it will respond in this manner only by accident. In the category of independently variable items would come almost all new long-term investments, repayment of loans in advance of maturity, and many services.

The factors principally conditioning long-term international loans are differences between national markets in long-term interest rates and in the prospect of profits at home and abroad. Such differences remain for long periods pretty much the same regardless of the changes in the international accounts. (The latter changes tend to be results rather than causes of such variations as may occur in international long-term lending and borrowing.) Long-term lenders and investment banking houses quite properly leave to the commercial bankers the task of accommodation to a tendency toward an excess of foreign claims over domestic counter claims, and proceed with their operations whether or not those operations will increase the tendency toward disequilibrium.[25] There is little if any inducement for them, in

[25] A long-term loan is, however, sometimes deferred, or even transferred to another lending market, when there is a "tight" *banking* situation in the prospective lending country and the connection between banking and investment houses is close. A stringency in the banking situation, with temporarily high short-term money rates, tends to recur in lending countries whenever the scale of long-term lending is extended, since such an extension usually leads, in the first instance, to an outward drain of gold. This tightness in short-term money markets is by no means to be confused with inability of residents of the country concerned to lend. It is more frequently evidence of a very great ability. High short-term money rates are likely to be a fairly regular *result* of so low a rate of interest on long-term loans as to prompt heavy foreign investments. Conversely, countries in which the banks have large gold reserves, and where low short interest rates therefore prevail, are by no means necessarily likely to engage in heavy international long-term investment.

the tendency toward disequilibrium in the international accounts or the corollaries thereof, to adopt any other policy. The same can be said with regard to repayment of loans by former borrowers before the date nominated in the bond. Important service items, such as total freight payments and tourist trade, are also but very loosely correlated with changes in the status of the international accounts as a whole. This is likewise true of most of the *miscellaneous* unilateral items.

Under normal conditions, the most highly variable and, at the same time, appropriately elastic item in the international accounts is short-term international indebtedness. A shift in the relationship in any country between claims and counter claims on other items is, in the first instance, likely to be compensated by an opposite change of equal magnitude in the short-term international borrowing or lending of that country. The adjustment is, for moderate amounts, so easy as to be, at first, almost insensible. It occurs through a shift in banking funds from one international center to another as a result of paying out funds in one monetary medium, in exchange for receipts in another, in the purchase and sale of bills of exchange.

Banks require, however, a more or less fixed distribution of their funds as between the domestic and foreign markets, and when this distribution is disturbed by exchange operations they will alter their exchange rate quotations in an attempt to restore the desired relationship. The banks, and particularly the central bank, in the country to which the exchange rate movement is adverse will also ordinarily raise the discount rate (bank rate of interest) and this will tend to draw in further short-term funds. All this furthers immediate equilibrium in the international accounts. Under abnormal conditions, however, where fear plays a great part, the movement of short-term funds may not respond to changes in interest rates or it may respond inappropriately. The movement of short-term funds, far from effecting equilibrium, may then be of major importance in exaggerating disequilibrium.[26]

───────────

[26] In the critical situation of recent years, for instance, a sharp rise in a central bank interest rate has, often with good reason, been

Even in comparatively normal situations where the tendency toward disequilibrium, though momentarily slight, is thoroughgoing, the minor movement in exchange rates possible under gold standards, and the raising of the rate of interest, will be inadequate to the attainment of equilibrium. Resort is then had to a transfer of gold. Such transfers are also a highly variable and appropriately elastic item in the international accounts.

If, as a result of free currency standards, gold is not available at a fixed rate in the currency of the country against which foreign claims are tending to outrun counter claims, exchange rates will have to alter until a temporary, and eventually a stable, equilibrium in the international accounts is achieved. With or without gold standards, *stable* equilibrium is likely to come only through a more or less permanent shift in the relationship between commodity exports and imports[27] which are the third

interpreted as a danger signal preliminary to abandonment of the gold standard and restrictions on withdrawal of funds. Instead of attracting short-term deposits it has therefore led rather to a "run" on the currency of the country in question. Short-term funds have been withdrawn from countries where so much as 15 per cent interest was offered, to be deposited in countries where only one per cent was to be obtained.

[27] Along with a shift in such service items as respond in an appropriately elastic direction. The principal service item in the American international account is "tourism." This is in part appropriately elastic and in part independently mobile. There may, no doubt, be some increase in American travel abroad when, as a result of a tendency toward excess of American claims on foreigners over the counter claims, foreign prices fall in terms of American currency. Such an increase in American foreign travel would augment foreign counter claims on American currency and so operate to restore stable equilibrium. In the main, however, American tourist traffic, both ways, is largely independent of relative prices in the United States and abroad. The balance of income and outlay on this item fluctuates in response to quite other causes, principally the state of general economic well-being in the United States; and there would, in any case, be almost no tendency toward appropriate adjustment except where free currencies, either in the United States or abroad, are involved.

and most important of the appropriately elastic items in the adjustment of disequilibria.

Gold movements are convenient emergency resources, excellent shock absorbers, but they are, by their very nature, impermanently operative in any one direction. Shifts in merchandise movements are slower to occur, but ultimate reliance must be placed on changes in the ratio of ordinary commodity exports to imports to compensate any deviation from equilibrium in the other items. Aside from temporary adjustments through short-term loans, the movement of gold or of exchange rates must continue in response to a deep-lying lack of equilibrium until it is sufficient so to alter the relationship between prices or monetary purchasing power in the several countries as to bring about in each such shifts in the ratio of commodity exports to imports as will, when all items are included, lead to an equality of claims and counter claims in current international accounts.

The great permanent make-weight, the fundamental equilibrator, in the international account is, therefore, commodity trade. All other important and permanently effective items being independently determined, any more or less permanent deviation from parity of claims and counter claims which occurs in these items is automatically balanced by an opposite deviation from parity in merchandise transactions. Whatever the *total* volume of exports and of imports, the spread between them must therefore, over any reasonably extended period, maintain a constant relationship of equality with the spread, in the opposite direction, between claims and counter claims arising from other permanent items in the international account.[28] At any given time and under any given status of the fixed and the independently determined mobile items, commodity exports and imports are therefore tied together. An increase in commodity exports thus involves an equal increase in commodity imports,

---

[28] Temporary items such as gold movements, and short-term loans, must eventually be canceled by counter movements of gold or repayment of the loans or else must change their character and take a place among the permanent items calling for compensation in *commodity* trade.

and an increase in commodity imports will automatically give rise to a corresponding augmentation of commodity exports. The same is of course true of decreases.

This conclusion, as noted in the text, is of superlative importance in a consideration of commercial policy since it means that the most drastic measures in curtailment of commodity imports will, in the degree in which they are effective, merely reduce commodity exports in equal measure. Similarly, the utmost energy devoted to promoting export trade in goods cannot overcome the effect of a restriction of imports and will not succeed in changing the spread between commodity exports and commodity imports which results from other items in the international account. It may, if not checked by rigid import restrictions, increase both exports and imports but it will not increase the one at the expense of the other. The restrictions on imports imposed by many countries in the last few years in an attempt to relieve unemployment, have for this reason been quite nugatory for the purpose for which they were intended and have, in other ways, been extremely harmful. The passion for exports, and the efforts to promote them without a willingness to receive a corresponding volume of imports, are open to the same condemnation. Exports as an outlet for a falsely conceived "surplus" of general productive power are a broken reed. Their only real function is to serve as a payment for present or prospective imports which are not a curse but a national blessing. The volume of employment is not affected by the volume of imports. However large the latter may be there is, in the fact itself, no reason to expect unemployment in the importing country since exports will soon develop *pari passu* with any expansion of imports. Restraints on imports may possibly prevent for the moment a drain of gold but, if so, they are likely to perpetuate the condition they are designed to combat.

Control of foreign trade, to prevent a drain of gold or a fall in the exchange value of the currency of the country resorting to such measures, far from effecting any definitive remedy of a maladjustment, exaggerates its importance. Such control reduces the possibility of export through forcing foreigners to pay, in their own currency, for the goods of the country of control a much higher price than would otherwise be necessary. At the same time it increases the domestic demand for imports by keeping the domestic price level relatively high or the purchasing power of the domestic currency over foreign goods greater than an equilibrium position warrants. The effects of such measures are therefore perverse in the extreme. Here, as elsewhere in the phenomena of international trade, control tends to defeat its own ends.

Lightning Source UK Ltd.
Milton Keynes UK
UKHW021319271121
394660UK00003B/319